HIRE FOR GRIT

HIRE FOR GRIT

HIRE GREAT TALENT, CREATE OPPORTUNITY & CHANGE LIVES

RAJ N. SUCHAK

HIRE FOR GRIT

HIRE GREAT TALENT, CREATE OPPORTUNITY & CHANGE LIVES

ISBN   978-1-63676-827-4   *Paperback*

          978-1-63730-215-6   *Kindle Ebook*

          978-1-63730-271-2   *Ebook*

"To be gritty is to keep putting one foot in front of the other. To be gritty is to hold fast to an interesting and purposeful goal. To be gritty is to invest, day after week after year, in challenging practice. To be gritty is to fall down seven times, and rise eight."

ANGELA LEE DUCKWORTH

To dearest Sharon, you bring
balance to everything I do.

To dearest Nikki & Dylan, you inspire
me every day to live a life of example.

To my dearest parents, I am grateful for
your unconditional love & support.

CONTENTS

———

INTRODUCTION

——

Growing up, I was always encouraged to dream big and join the entrepreneurial journey that my ancestors before had pursued. In 2011, I finally decided to take the leap of faith. With minimal savings, a second child on the way, and no other form of income, I started Cloud62, a technical consulting company. The idea was simple: Cloud62 would help companies implement Salesforce.com for their organization. When an organization buys enterprise software, like Salesforce.com, they often need consulting expertise that customizes the software to their specific business. That is where Cloud62 came in. We helped organizations create custom setups and best practices unique to them.

With little money, a big heart, and a "can-do" attitude, I jumped into the highly competitive and fast-growing technical consulting industry. The first order of business was hiring the right people. But I had a problem. Talent was hard to come by, expensive, and heavily pursued by competitors.

Our competition could pay more. Our competition had richer benefits. Our competition even had break rooms with foosball tables and beer on tap. We were frugal, sometimes overly frugal. We furnished our offices with used furniture. Our health insurance plan could hardly classify as a "benefit." We were tadpoles competing in a sea of sharks in one of the most challenging environments for talent. We had to think differently, if we wanted to succeed.

That's when I first met Pete.

Pete worked as a pastry chef at a highly-rated Italian restaurant in Buffalo, NY. He had worked for twelve years perfecting the art of making pastries. Pete was responsible for all the desserts and became an important part of the head chef's team to ensure customers had a wonderful culinary experience. Pete was often the first one in the restaurant and prepped for the baking that needed to be done for the day. He would go into the kitchen and work alone for hours before anyone else showed up. Pete was trusted and respected by his team to get the job done before they came in. If for any reason Pete didn't deliver his part, a chain reaction of chaos could follow. But that rarely happened because Pete was not the type of person to let people down.

During his time as a pastry chef, Pete lived with four roommates because he couldn't afford his own place. He barely made past minimum wage. Pete would take the bus to work, even in the Buffalo winters, because he couldn't afford a car.

Growing up, Pete had his own way of learning in school. His nonconformist attitude made it harder for him to fit in. In school, he quickly learned on his own; he would question more than others and he would tinker and try versus just regurgitating classroom material. Pete learned more through discovery by merely trying. Because of Pete's unique style of learning, he needed extra attention. His school didn't have the resources to accommodate different learning styles.

Eventually, Pete dropped out of high school. He couldn't conform. Pete decided to make his own path forward.

After dropping out, Pete worked odd jobs in restaurants like a pizza shop, Chinese takeout and other fast-food establishments to make ends meet. When Pete wasn't working, he would tinker and spend countless hours working on his hobbies. He was always fascinated by how things worked; what made them work; how they could break; and how they could be improved. An always curious Pete was constantly working with computers. He often made his own computer using recycled parts found in electronic recycle dumpsters.

As time went on, days became weeks, and weeks became years and Pete settled into a routine as a pastry chef taking great pride in his work. He beamed with joy at the end of every shift. He took pleasure in doing his part and setting the foundation for the day's culinary success at the restaurant.

My company, Cloud62, was growing and we wanted to hire people that believed in our vision of always going the extra mile for our customers.

I still remember the day I was introduced to Pete. He was the roommate of one of the team members at Cloud62. When I received his resume, I immediately looked him up on LinkedIn. Pete's photo consisted of him shirtless, with a colorful mohawk holding a piece of steak up to his face. At first glance, this was not a technical company's dream candidate. His resume had no formal technical education or experience listed. The only mention of technology was that he liked working with computers.

My immediate reaction was: No way! Customers pay us top dollar and expect a certain level of professionalism. I thought:

How could I justify hiring a person with no formal education to be a billable consultant?

What would my customers think if they ever looked Pete up?

What would my customers think if they found out that Pete had dropped out of high school and worked as a pastry chef for twelve years?

Would they consider hiring us as consultants with someone like Pete on the team?

I had a big problem. We were growing fast! I had trouble finding competent individuals I could afford. We did hire some unconventional people in the past, many of whom ended up being good hires. So, even though I was inclined to say no immediately, I thought maybe there was a chance that I could train Pete to do some of the menial duties and keep him behind the curtains when it came to customer service.

I invited Pete to an in-person interview thinking he would show up with his mohawk and some sort of punk fashion style. I was wrong. Pete walked into my office with a neat haircut and dressed in a suit. I was surprised. I could tell Pete was nervous. He had never interviewed in a professional setting before. He had sweaty palms and spoke quickly, trying hard to impress. Pete saw this as an opportunity that he didn't want to mess up.

I was candid with Pete that we were not like any other places where he had worked before. Cloud62 didn't have the structure or processes in place to formally train people. Pete would have to learn proactively mostly on his own and ask for specific help when he ran into roadblocks. There was no formal training program or a classroom setting where Pete would get to learn for a few months in a sandbox environment. The first six months at Cloud62 would be like jumping into the ocean in the middle of a hurricane with great white sharks circling while you barely knew how to swim. Giving Pete a chance boiled down to timing and desperation because we were extremely under-staffed. It was exceptionally challenging to find talent who knew Salesforce. com in Buffalo. In turn, we often resorted to hiring if we believed the person could learn quickly.

After the interview pleasantries, I wanted to see how Pete could work on problems that didn't have a clear answer. The goal of the interview exercise was to see if Pete could logically think through problems. Did he give up easily when posed with a question that he couldn't answer? Was Pete naturally curious? Would Pete be comfortable being uncomfortable? I was very surprised with Pete's ability to think through problems and use his life experiences to solve the issues I presented to him. I wasn't looking for a right or wrong answer; what mattered was Pete's willingness to attempt the problems and whether or not he gave it his best effort.

I was impressed with Pete. He was very engaged throughout the interview and we wanted to give Pete a chance to work at Cloud62, *but* first he had to prove to us that he would take this opportunity seriously. Pete was given our disorganized recruiting case study and pointers on free learning resources he could use to complete it. Pete took on the challenge.

The Cloud62 recruiting case study was a scrappy, quickly written document, at best, with limited information and pointers to online resources that anyone could access and learn from. The case study had many gaps and holes, some by design, but many because we simply didn't invest the time that we should have in preparing it. The goal of the case study was *not* to see whether the candidate got it right or wrong. The goal was about seeing if the candidate had the curiosity to learn and take something that wasn't structured and make sense of it. We wanted to see *how* the candidate thought through the problem.

In 2014, Salesforce.com skills were in high demand (they still are) and the demand for talent greatly outmatched the available resources. Given the nature disruption that cloud software fueled for enterprises, IDC (International Data Corporation) projected over three million new jobs by 2022 with billions of dollars in economic impact created globally![1] Companies couldn't hire talent fast enough so they turned to consultants like Cloud62. The problem was, we couldn't hire fast enough either and had to resort to hiring differently.

To add to the severe shortage of talent, companies like Microsoft, Google, Facebook and others were also creating technical ecosystems that were growing like wildfire. Forester Research concluded that the economic savings for organizations moving to the Microsoft cloud were in the tens of millions of dollars, and, as a result, organizations were moving to the cloud in droves![2] To support the transition there was an extreme need for talent, and yet the shortage was only getting worse.[3]

---

1. John F. Gantz, *The Salesforce Economy Forecast: 3.3 Million New Jobs and $859 Billion New Business Revenue to Be Created from 2016 to 2022* (Framingham, MA: International Data Corporation, 2017), 1-3.
2. Sean Owens, *The Total Economic Impact™ of Microsoft Azure IaaS: Cost Savings, New Revenue Opportunities, and Business Benefits Enabled by Azure IaaS* (Cambridge, MA: Forrester Research, 2017), 1.
3. Kim S. Nash, "CIOs Get Clever about Finding Needed Skills as IT Talent Shortage Grows," *CIO Blog, Wall Street Journal*, May 19, 2015.

Over the next couple of weeks, Pete started learning Salesforce.com. Like everything he pursued, he dove in headfirst! Occasionally we would get questions from him as he learned and tried to relate his learnings to the case study. The questions showed two things: (1) he was still pursuing the goal of providing an answer to the case study, and (2) he was a self-starter who could learn on his own. Both were excellent indicators that Pete would be a great fit for Cloud62.

We invited Pete back to the office so he could present his case study to our team. This time, I was more hopeful that Pete was going to be a good fit for Cloud62 given his efforts over the last two weeks. As he began his presentation, we noticed that he felt comfortable in tense situations. He was passionate, articulate, and had clearly done his homework on Salesforce.com.

Looking back, I can see how my conscious bias made me overlook the potential in Pete. We would have never been able to see what Pete was capable of just by looking at his work experience and educational background.

In fact, it's not just about work experience and educational background that can lead to bias. Recent studies at UCLA, Harvard Business School, and UPenn found that our names can also lead to bias![4, 5, 6] In particular, the UPenn[7] study shows that names that are highly indicative of race

---

4. "UCLA Study Suggests Researchers Look More Closely at Connections between Names and Race," UCLA Newsroom press release, September 8, 2017, on the UCLA Newsroom website, written by Jessica Wolf.

5. Dina Gerdman, "Minorities Who 'Whiten' Job Resumes Get More Interviews," *Working Knowledge* (blog), *Harvard Business School*, May 17, 2017.

6. Judd B. Kesler, Corinne Low, and Colin D. Sullivan. "Incentivized Resume Rating: Eliciting Employer Preferences without Deception," *National Bureau of Economic Research* (May 2019): 4-6.

7. Ibid.

and gender leads to bias in the recruiting process. Richard Tsao, Reshawn Washington, Andres Barajas, and Kyle Wood are such examples that are respectively indicative of Asian, African American, Hispanic and White males. That is just one other example of biases that are formed.

"How many other Petes are out there?" "How many Petes haven't gotten a fair chance?"

Once we hired Pete, we were blown away by what he did at Cloud62 every day. Pete quickly became the go-to guy for many of the challenges that needed fixing at our start-up. We needed help with technical problems and Pete came to the rescue. The important contributions that Pete made were not based on his job description. They were simply based on Pete seeing a problem that needed fixing and then without permission jumping in headfirst to fix it. The years he spent, as a pastry chef, assisting the head chef, taught him valuable skills about how to work on a team and the importance of never letting the team down.

Can you imagine if I had let my biases prevent me from hiring Pete? Could it be that there are millions of people globally that are never given a chance because of conscious and unconscious biases? What can we do to reduce bias and democratize opportunities for all?

At Cloud62, we hired over thirty people using a new approach we call "Hire for Grit." This book is about creating a framework that allows other companies to do the same. *Hire for Grit* helped us compete as a small company and aided in our continued growth! *Hire for Grit* at Cloud62 helped us stay one step ahead, while making a difference in the lives of our team members. We're going to take a look at what Cloud62 did, our long-term impact, and how you can do the same. If a small company like ours with limited resources can make a difference, imagine what could happen if larger companies tried the *Hire for Grit* approach.

The *Hire for Grit* framework is based on four core beliefs:

1. There are millions of underemployed people (people with the potential to do more than the work they do every day.)
2. Organizations must create equal opportunity for all without bias when hiring.
3. We live in a world where access to information is no longer the core problem to learn and grow.
4. Hiring for character is more important for the long term than hiring for skill.

In this book, we will explore each of those beliefs and outline practical steps organizations can take to hire for grit. Anyone in search of talent, from visionary CEOs to hiring managers can hire better and faster using the principles outlined in this book. If you are a talent acquisition professional who is open to new ideas and tired of being constrained by the lack of talent, this book is for you.

Let's get started!

PART 1

GRIT & HIRING

——

CHAPTER 1

HOW WE HIRE TODAY

———

Hiring is hard! For most hiring managers, recruiting for their team is one of their biggest pain points and yet, a top priority. Say you are a manager and need to hire someone for your team. What process should you follow? What should you expect? The hiring process typically includes the following steps:

- Convincing management that there is a real need for the requisition and getting approval for it
- Crafting the right job description and criteria to evaluate applicants
- Posting the job online (or working with an outside agency) and waiting for candidates and resumes
- Reaching out to personal networks to see if anyone they know is looking for a new opportunity
- Vetting resumes and applicants
- Reviewing vetted applicants and coordinating with members of the team to get their feedback
- Phone screening and interviewing candidates
- Deciding to hire or not to hire based on the applicant's interview performance and the team's feedback

- Working through the offer process and convincing the candidate to join their team if they have more than one offer on the table

Wow! That is a lot of hurdles to jump through and it can be incredibly complex. According to the Bureau of Labor Statistics as of November 2020, there are over six hundred thousand open jobs in America and that number has been consistently higher than six hundred thousand in the months prior.[8] If companies generally follow the above process, consider how big of a challenge hiring is and yet, according to Predictive Index, hiring is considered a top priority for most CEOs and executives.[9]

The challenges associated with hiring people can be broken down into three broad categories.

1. Hiring is time consuming and expensive
2. Hiring is biased and error prone
3. Hiring creates poor experiences

Let's review each of the challenges in greater detail.

Hiring is Time Consuming and Expensive

According to the Society for Human Resources Management (SHRM) Human Capital Report the average time to fill a

---

8. U.S. Bureau of Labour Statistics, *Job Openings Levels and Rates by Industry and Region, Seasonally Adjusted,* last modified February 9, 2021, Economic News Release distributed by U.S. Bureau of Labour Statistics.

9. Thad Peterson, "Top CEO Priorities in 2019," *Consultant Resources* (blog), *The Predictive Index,* accessed February 28, 2021.

position is thirty-six days, the cost per hire is $4,425 and the annual overall turnover rate is 38 percent.[10] That means that after a job requisition has been approved, the average time to find and hire the right person takes over a month and operationally costs an organization a significant amount when you factor in advertising, travel, coordination and personnel costs. Those numbers can be even higher for certain industries like technology and healthcare. Organizations spend an incredible amount of time and money in recruiting the right talent just to lose 38 percent of that talent after the first year.

If the hiring process is expensive, making the wrong decision on who to hire is even more so. In the early days of Amazon.com, Jeff Bezos was asked about his hiring approach. He said, "I'd rather interview fifty people and not hire anyone than hire the wrong person." The Department of Labor estimates the cost of a bad hire to be 30 percent of their annual compensation. So, making the wrong hiring decision adds to the high cost of hiring people in the first place.[11] However, this does not include the intangible cost of hiring the wrong person in terms of team morale, productivity and other meaningful measures. Hiring the right person can provide a well-functioning team, a strong and thriving culture and a collaborative environment that encourages hiring better than oneself.

At Cloud62 and even later at Huron Consulting Group, I experienced the disruption created by a wrong hire. The wrong hiring decision often meant that we had to deal with slipping timelines, cost overruns on projects, a drop in employee morale and unhappy customers. Thanks to our

10. Andrew Mariotti et. al, *2017 Talent Acquisition Benchmarking Report*, (Alexandria, VA: Society for Human Resource, 2017), 4-15.
11. Northwestern University, "The Cost of a Bad Hire," *Northwestern*, February 2019.

stringent hiring process, the wrong hiring decisions were a rarity. Still, they resulted in a negative impact throughout the organization.

And what about the cost of not hiring on time? If you take a look at the organization's revenue per employee and divide that by the number of working days in the calendar year, you get the cost of not hiring on time for each day. For example, the revenue per employee for the energy industry is one million seven hundred thousand dollars and assuming two hundred twenty working days in a year, for each day that an energy company does not hire, the cost is a staggering seven thousand seven hundred dollars. The daily cost of not hiring on time for the healthcare industry is four thousand and fifty dollars.[12]

Recruiting costs can also go up when there isn't enough talent available to hire. I recently spoke to Alicia Kenney, the VP of HR at BryLin Hospital. She, like many other HR executives, is constantly on the lookout for healthcare talent and works hard every day to ensure the talent they have is retained. Alicia and many other executives at hospitals, nursing homes, and managed care facilities have an "always hiring" policy to ensure they are keeping up with the need to be fully staffed. For healthcare organizations, hiring for registered nurses (RNs), certified nurse aides (CNAs) and license practical nurses (LPNs) is a constant challenge. A simple search on job boards like Indeed for a registered nurse (RN) position yield over 170,000 job openings.

In summary, the cost of hiring is dictated by the time it takes to hire, hiring the right person, and ensuring that there

---

12. Jeff Desjardins, *Which Companies Make the Most Revenue per Employee?* (Vancouver, BC: Visual Capitalist, 2017), figure 1.

is a talent pool available to hire from. For most organizations, reducing the time to hire and putting checks and balances in place to hire right are two of the best ways to reduce the cost of hiring.

Hiring is Biased and Error Prone

Hiring is biased. According to UPenn's team of researchers, biases exist in most steps of the hiring process.[13] From writing job descriptions, to resume evaluations and interpreting a candidate's fit for the role, biases based on gender, name, employment status and other factors are a common occurrence in the recruiting process. In addition to bias, errors can also arise when the hiring process is not consistently defined and implemented.

What can organizations do to reduce bias and errors when hiring?

Job descriptions can be exclusionary

According to SHRM, starting with job descriptions is a good place.[14] The goal of job descriptions is to articulate what the role entails and the responsibilities of the position. Also, job descriptions describe the educational, experience

---

13. Wharton University, "Uncovering Bias: A New Way to Study Hiring Can Help," *Knowledge@Wharton* (blog), *Wharton School of the University of Pennsylvania*, July 18, 2019.

14. Rebecca Knight, "7 Practical Ways to Reduce Bias in Your Hiring Process," *Talent Acquisition* (blog), *Society for Human Resource Management*, April 19, 2018.

requirements of the roles and set the right expectations for the candidates that are interested in applying. In some ways, job descriptions are used by companies to ensure that only qualified people apply. However, who determines if they are qualified? Number of years of experience? Educational background? The candidate themselves? The recruiter? Can job descriptions increase bias and reduce candidate diversity?

According to the Journal of Personality and Social Psychology the use of certain male dominated words in job descriptions significantly reduces the likelihood of women applying for the role.[15] Examples of such male dominated words in technology job descriptions are "ninja," "champion," and others. For a full list of male and feminine oriented words that organizations should be mindful of, see https://www.hiremorewomenintech.com/.

Qualifications limit the pool

In addition to the words used in the job description, the "qualifications" part of the job description can also lead to bias and error in judgement when considering candidates. Research has shown that men apply for a job when they meet at least 60 percent of the qualifications, while women tend to apply if they meet 100 percent of the qualifications.[16] Cre-

---

15. Danielle Gaucher, Justin Friesen, and Aaron C. Kay, "Evidence That Gendered Wording in Job Advertisements Exists and Sustains Gender Inequality," *Journal of Personality and Social Psychology* 101, no. 1 (January 2011): 109-28.

16. Tara Sophia Mohr, "Why Women Don't Apply for Jobs Unless They're 100% Qualified," *Harvard Business Review*, August 25, 2014.

ating qualification criteria that is overly selective can sway a candidate pool's gender diversity.

The qualifications part of a job description not only leads to bias, but the actual qualifications are often times just a guess of what is required. For example, if a job description has five years of experience as one of the requirements for the role, could someone with three years of experience truly be less qualified? Years of work experience is a prime example of how arbitrary criteria can turn away qualified candidates and reduce diversity.

Biases associated with job descriptions are just the tip of the iceberg. Resumes are also a big source of bias in the hiring process.

Are resumes even relevant?

For starters, candidates and recruiters often play the *resume keyword game.*

Given the limited resources and time to review all applications for a position, a recruiter may be forced to quickly *scan* for keywords across the resumes received for the position. Candidates are well aware of that strategy and often create a resume packed with keywords that may result in their resume showing up on a recruiter's radar. This approach to zeroing in on the right candidate is fundamentally flawed because a candidate may jam pack their resume with the right keywords for it to be picked up by a biased algorithm or recruiter while other more qualified candidates may never even be considered. As a candidate, knowing how to play the *resume keyword game* means that you are likely to be on top of the stack while people who may be more qualified or capable may never get their chance.

To reduce dependence on keywords, some companies leverage the power of case studies in hiring talent. McKinsey & Company (considered one of the most successful consulting organizations in the world) is known to hire from the top schools and gets thousands of candidates who apply for their associate position.

According to Caitlin Storhaug, leader of McKinsey's global recruiting programs, "[McKinsey] recruits from the programs that everyone has heard about like Wharton, Stanford and MIT but also from other schools around the world that might have a really excellent program in something we are looking for, like a great engineering, digital or agriculture program."[17] Kerry Casey is the Director of Americas Recruiting for McKinsey. Casey explains, "We look for analytical people who want to create positive results for our clients."[18] An important part of the hiring process at McKinsey involves a case exercise that qualified candidates are asked to work on and present to the hiring team. The case study helps hiring teams see how a candidate analyzes and logically thinks and communicates to help them determine how they could perform in front of clients.

The larger question is, does a resume really represent a candidate? Just like how a traditional job description can't fully represent and describe what it is like to work at a company, resumes are a poor way to create more than a 'one-dimensional' view of a candidate. Not only is it hard to get to know the candidate in order for a company to make an

---

17. Abigail Johnson Hess, "How to Land a Job at Mckinsey," *Make It* (blog), *CNBC*, June 6, 2018.

18. Ibid.

informed decision, but it is hard for the candidate to truly demonstrate and explain why they are the right fit for the role. Resumes can also lead to conscious or subconscious biases. Biases can arise based on names, gender and other identifiable information that can easily be gleamed from a resume. According to researchers at Harvard and Princeton University's department of economics, female musicians, in the past, have faced discrimination when applying for symphony orchestra jobs if the musician isn't given a chance to demonstrate their capabilities.[19] If *blind* auditions were used in the evaluation process such that a candidate gender and name were not revealed there was a substantial increase in female musician new hires.

So what can we learn from that? One strategy an organization can use is to remove references to names, gender, and other identifiable information and give every single candidate the same chance to demonstrate their fit for the role. It's a step in the right direction, yet bias can still creep into the process when a candidate meets face-to-face with the company.

Another strategy to reduce bias is to remove dependence on the same types of backgrounds and qualifications from the pool of candidates that the organization has hired from. Some of the top companies in the world take a very proactive approach to reducing bias this way. At Goldman Sachs, one would expect them to hire people with top financial backgrounds. However, according to a recruiter (name withheld) who worked in Goldman Sachs securities division, people that have demonstrated excellence in economics

19. Claudia Goldin and Cecelia Rouse, "Orchestrating Impartiality: The Impact of 'Blind' Auditions on Female Musicians," *American Economic Review* 90, no. 4 (September 2000): 715-741.

and financial internships are not necessarily the most ideal candidates.[20] They are considered *plug and play* candidates who are not exciting. Goldman Sachs prefers to hire people with unusual and diverse profiles. If you have a background in English Literature and have demonstrated success, you are just as likely to be considered as someone who has a finance degree with top grades. At Goldman, there is a big emphasis on character and the pursuit of excellence. Grades and a top school background are a step in the right direction, but long-term ambition is at the heart of the decision-making process.

For technology companies like Google, the hiring process and decision making is unique with the ultimate goal of reducing bias. According to Lisa Stern Hayes, Google's global staffing lead and senior recruiter, a hiring manager can say *no* to a candidate for any reason, but the final *yes* must be a decision that is approved by the hiring committee.[21] A hiring manager alone cannot give the final *yes* to hiring someone. According to Hayes, "Research tell us that teams that have diverging opinions can make better less biased decisions." Hiring decisions can be slowed down by leveraging a team consensus approach, and rushing a decision could also lead to making biased decisions. According to Hayes, a bad hire can have "long lasting negative effects on a team or a company's culture."[22]

---

20. Clive Smith, "I Was a Recruiter for Goldman Sachs. Here's Who They Want to Hire," *eFinancialCareers* (blog), May 5, 2016.
21. Ruth Umoh, "Top Google Recruiter: Google Uses This 'Shocking' Strategy to Hire the Best Employees," *Make It* (blog), *CNBC*, January 10, 2018.
22. Ibid.

Hiring leads to Poor Experiences

The number one complaint by candidates when applying for a job is that they never hear back from the organization after they have put in the time and energy in the recruiting process. Sometimes the *apply and wait* phenomenon is also referred to as a *recruiting black hole*. Often when candidates do hear back, it is in the form of a generic response acknowledging receipt of the application or a rejection notice a few weeks after.

Over the last few years, many job boards have created a *one-click* application process to make it easier for the candidates to apply. As a result, recruiters get far more applicants than they can handle for a role and the 'apply and wait' phenomenon has become more prevalent. There is no doubt that organizations need to do more to get back to candidates. This is not easy. Without using automation and technology to create personalized experiences for candidates, organizations simply can't respond to all candidates. According to Tim Mayer, Director of Talent Acquisition for Kraus-Anderson Construction Company, "The sheer volume of applications makes it difficult to notify all candidates that they are no longer being considered for a role."[23]

For most candidates, in addition to the wait time, lack of feedback from an organization creates a poor experience. Ideally, candidates expect one or more reasons why they are not being considered for the role. The challenge again is that organizations simply cannot respond to each and every candidate with a customized reason why they are not

---

23. Matt Krumrie, "Why Candidates Never Hear Back from Hiring Managers," *Zip Recruiter Blog*, July 6, 2015.

being considered. The high volume of responses is one reason it's hard to give feedback. More importantly, organizations have to make a call about the worthiness of the applicant by looking at their resume or cover letter (or both) and giving feedback about that is even harder.

The emotional stress can be a significant factor for candidates when they don't hear back from organizations they have applied to. Not hearing back can result in a loss of self-esteem and a feeling of resentment towards the organization.

What about the recruiter's experience? Is that any better? Once the job is posted online, recruiters can get inundated with an avalanche of resumes and cover letters. The number is often far too high to be able to give each applicant the amount of time required to properly review their candidacy, leading to the use of keywords. Recruiters know that their methods for reviewing the slew of resumes isn't the best; nonetheless, they search for keywords when faced with the enormous task of sifting through thousands of resumes. The recruiters, during this stage, can be overwhelmed and stressed, making for a poor experience.

Once the recruiters have narrowed down their potential candidates, it is time for them to begin the phone screening process. The list of candidates for the phone screening can be long, and it can take a considerable amount of time. Recruiters often describe their phone screenings as a leap of faith, as they only know some basic information about the candidate. Choosing the wrong candidates to phone screen costs time and money. Coordinating a convenient time to do these screenings can be a laborious and stressful process. After creating a short list of candidates, a recruiter works closely with the hiring manager to zero in on the right one.

But, what kind of an experience does this lead to for the hiring manager?

Hiring managers and recruiters often butt heads. Hiring managers may have unreasonable expectations given the constraints like pay, geography, experience etc., while expecting recruiters to know and understand the complexities of the qualifications to give them more qualified candidates. The gap that exists in expectations and understanding the fit for the role often originates from the job description, which is what the recruiter uses to vet and create a short list of candidates.

We can see the current hiring processes organizations use creates poor experiences for candidates, recruiters and hiring managers.

Is there anything we can do to make the process less expensive, less biased, more inclusive and create better experiences? The answer is YES! There is a better way to hire that addresses many of the challenges we discussed.

In the next chapter, we explore what "grit" means so we can get to what it means to "Hire for Grit."

CHAPTER 2

UNDERSTANDING GRIT

———

The lynchpin for this book is the word "grit", but what does that mean and why is that relevant?

There is no better person to answer that question than Angela Duckworth, Professor at the University of Pennsylvania and faculty co-director of the Penn-Wharton Behavior Change for Good Initiative. Angela gave a TEDx Talk about grit that has garnered millions of views.[24] She also wrote a book called *Grit: The Power of Passion and Perseverance.*[25] There are many definitions of grit however, Angela coined this one:

> "Grit is demonstrated passion and perseverance for long term goals."
>
> DR. ANGELA DUCKWORTH, PROFESSOR,
> UNIVERSITY OF PENNSYLVANIA

———

24. Angela Duckworth, "Grit: The Power of Passion and Perseverance," filmed April 2013 in New York, NY, TED video, 2:55.
25. Angela Duckworth, *Grit: The Power of Passion and Perseverance* (New York: Charles Scribner's Sons, 2016), 1.

Duckworth's research at University of Pennsylvania has shown a direct correlation between grit and educational success, military retention, spelling bee competitions, and personal pursuits.

Duckworth and her team at the Character Lab at UPenn have created a playbook for people to assess their grit level and provide tips on how to identify it.[26] This research also includes a self-assessment grit scale that helps one identify factors like distraction, setbacks, goal setting, hard work, focus, completion, and diligence in determining one's "grittiness."

James Clear, the best-selling author of *Atomic Habits,* thinks of grit as "mental toughness" and outlines many ways in which one can build the toughness via his book and blog.[27]

To understand what grit really means for someone personally, I recently interviewed Jason Arbegast.

If you ran into Jason, you would not think much of him. He is soft spoken, likes to keep to himself, and definitely does not stand out as a driven and motivated person.

Yet, if you dig deeper you will learn that Jason is made up of raw grit.

At thirty-eight, Jason lives in a small community in Maine with his wife and three children. When I spoke to Jason, he described it as his dream location. He lives about an hour outside of Portland in a quiet community, known for having four seasons, a good quality of life, and no traffic. Most importantly the community is a slow-paced environment, which doesn't compromise his work-life balance. This

26. Angela Duckworth, "Grit Passion and Perseverance for Long-Term Goals," Character Lab, accessed on February 28, 2021.

27. James Clear, "Grit: A Complete Guide on Being Mentally Tough," *James Clear* (blog), accessed on February 28, 2021.

perfect life didn't come easy to Jason. It was filled with hard work, struggle, pain, and anxiety.

Jason attended high school in Elmira, NY. Elmira was once a promising manufacturing town with its economic future dependent on a diverse group of manufacturers. In recent years, manufacturers have moved their operations to other states and out of the country. The shift in the jobs' landscape has left a lack of opportunity for its youth.

When Jason graduated from Elmira High School, he decided to take a semester off, travel, and experience a world outside of the one he knew growing up. He moved to California for six months and realized the fast paced, big city life wasn't for him. After much contemplation and no clear picture of what his future would look like, Jason ended up pursuing a degree in creative writing and philosophy at SUNY Oswego. SUNY Oswego is a small NY State College on the south eastern shores of Lake Ontario. When I asked him why he chose SUNY Oswego, Jason replied, "I wanted to go fishing often while in college." When I asked how many times he went fishing while studying, he smiled and responded "Zero!"

While in college full time, Jason worked at the local Wegmans, a grocery store with a diehard consumer fan base throughout the northeastern US. According to *Fortune* magazine's Best Companies to Work For, Wegmans often competes with the likes of companies like Google and Salesforce.com.[28] Imagine a grocery store, which can't offer its employees the financial compensation that high growth technology companies can, still being rated as a top choice by employees. I digress, let's get back to Jason. He worked in the meat, product, and deli department at Wegmans throughout college.

---

28. "100 Best Companies to Work for," Fortune, accessed on February 28, 2021.

After graduation, like many youths with a liberal arts college education, he struggled to find employment. So, he did what anyone would do and went back to work at a place he knew and felt comfortable at. Jason spent the next fifteen years at Wegmans struggling to make ends meet. On many occasions throughout his fifteen-year tenure, he applied for promotions, only to be turned down each time. Jason had fire deep in his belly that fueled his work ethic and drove him to continuously go above and beyond. But, he struggled to showcase it, especially in a large company environment. Jason has never been a successful interviewee. When I last spoke to Jason, he described feeling helpless with nothing to look forward to and barely anything to show for the fifteen years he spent at Wegmans repeatedly turned down for a promotion.

Jason is not one to quit and just accept it. With no options immediately available, he decided to spend time at the local department of the labor office. There he applied to hundreds of jobs that remotely matched his educational background and experience. He even spent hours taking professional career counseling tests that told him what careers he should pursue with his educational background and experience. Oddly enough, software developer kept popping up apart from him having no background in software development. In fact, he didn't even have a computer and was nowhere near close to being the technical wiz of the family that everyone goes to when they have computer problems. Based on the advice of a computer algorithm, Jason evaluated his options and decided to start learning computer programming.

With much enthusiasm, he bought an old laptop and started taking online courses and watching YouTube videos to learn how to become a software developer. While working full-time and with two kids at home, Jason had to manage his time carefully. He resorted to working on his laptop during his lunch breaks at Wegmans. It was during that time, that Jason got his first break.

Matt, a professional software developer at Cloud62, would often visit Wegmans during lunch for a sub. Wegmans makes the best subs and Jason was often the guy behind the counter making them. Over time, Matt became a regular customer of Jason's. He noticed how much time Jason would spend time on his computer when he went on break. On one occasion, Matt and Jason would talk about Cloud62 and how we were hiring people with Salesforce.com programming skills. Matt encouraged Jason to apply and work through the interview case study that Cloud62 used. Without any formal background in Salesforce.com, Jason decided to take on the challenge and started preparing. Jason struggled with learning Salesforce.com and completing the case study interview. Yet he never gave up. After a few weeks of trying, he completed the case study as best he could and submitted it. A few days later, Cloud62 called him for an interview.

Jason had no idea what to expect in the interview. It was his first real interview after applying to hundreds of jobs. He was nervous that his lack of experience and expertise with the Salesforce.com platform would be a problem. He interviewed with Matt, a few others from the Cloud62 team and me. About five minutes into the interview, I had to leave due to a customer commitment. Jason walked out of the interview thinking he had completely bombed it because I had walked out early and there was no way he would be offered a job at our company.

Let's stop and think about Jason's actions for a minute. He was stuck in a dead-end job, didn't have all the resources to progress, but he found what he did have access to and made the most of it. Jason held himself accountable to learning and growing, even during lunch breaks at work. He met a random stranger who told him about a company and technology that he hadn't heard of before and decided to challenge himself and apply for a job. He prepared the best he could for the interview and even though he felt very uncomfortable, he still went through the interview process.

Two days later, we offered Jason a position at Cloud62. Jason didn't have any formal Salesforce.com experience. That didn't matter to us. Jason didn't go to school and study computer science, which is what many software developers do. That didn't matter to us. Jason didn't even do exceptional in the interview and his case study was average. Still, that didn't matter to us. The single biggest reason we hired Jason was because of his GRIT. Jason chose to be uncomfortable and never stopped trying. Jason possessed a growth mindset. Most importantly, Jason showed passion and perseverance. To us that was incredible and we had to have him on our team.

When I spoke to Jason for this book, he revealed many stories that he was afraid to share at the time he got hired. He carried a bottle of Pepto Bismol with him because he was sick to his stomach and worried that someone at Cloud62 would find out that he was unqualified. Jason was a great learner and became one of our best hires and yet, he didn't give up learning. Jason used his nervousness and worry to fuel his appetite to learn and become better.

Jason has continued on the path of learning, discovery, and growing every day. He has spent five plus years working as a software developer on the Salesforce.com platform since his hire at Cloud62. Jason has worked on numerous projects and is often sought after by companies that are looking for Salesforce.com skilled talent. In fact, Jason regularly receives emails from recruiters trying to convince him to go work for their firm.

With Jason's permission, here is an email he sent to me detailing his feelings about the hiring process and being pigeonholed.

Hey Raj,

Thank you for the meeting earlier today...very nice to see you again! As always I remember things that could have been said and weren't and mostly they can be ignored. But one point I feel could be made that I don't think I conveyed was the feeling of hopelessness after realizing I spent nearly 15 years at a company and was going to go nowhere. And despite it not likely to go anywhere, it also felt completely unlikely to ever change. The region I lived in had little opportunity for job prospects, certainly not without some credentials. I felt completely pigeonholed...this was the only career I could ever have and it was already over, it was just going to continue for another 40 years. That feeling of being stuck is awful and doesn't go away even after you're 'unstuck.' Anytime I had applied for jobs, I was a resume or application and the only thing people would see was fifteen years in a retail setting and they would immediately cast it aside because it doesn't match the 'hard skills' they are looking for. One of the reasons I was always anxious at Cloud62/Huron was because if I failed, I didn't have a backup plan. I burned my bridge at Wegmans, had hard skills for very few jobs that could let me leave the region, and no savings to get by. If I couldn't make it at C62, I'd become just another resume, this time with a blemish in failing out of a job after just a few weeks or months, and not enough time spent to have demonstrated any growth or ability in this new field. That feeling of being forever pigeonholed and stuck is pretty soul crushing.

Additionally, I thought of one big thing companies can do to modify their hiring process...get rid of the computer algorithms. Since reaching a point where I'd say I'm qualified for a position, I have had this experience more than once: I apply for a job (often through LinkedIn, but could be anywhere); I wait a day or two and receive a form rejection so vague and impersonal that it is almost certainly a computer scanning for a CS degree and tossing my application aside; then a week or two later receive a message from the same company's internal recruiter saying they found my LinkedIn profile and want to set up time to discuss (personal enough to show they actually did research my LinkedIn qualifications and resume...seen enough of the generic ones to tell the difference). Those algorithms can't take everything into account, and it won't look good for the company to contact someone their computer has already turned down. It certainly won't build any confidence in the hiring abilities.

Use any of this in your notes if you wish...and best wishes going forward!

Jason

As we wrap up Jason's story, the question that I keep thinking is, how many other Jasons are out there and what are companies doing to find them? I am willing to place bets that there are hundreds of thousands of people who are stuck in dead-end jobs, who want to work hard and yet the current recruiting processes don't grant them an opportunity to thrive and grow.

CHAPTER 3

WHY GRIT MATTERS WHEN HIRING

———

When Richard Branson, the billionaire founder and global philanthropist of the Virgin Group, was asked how he created 400+ companies by hiring remarkable people, his response focused on "prioritizing character over the resume."[29] Virgin Group uses group interviews where applicants are asked to play games with one another allowing the hiring team to see a candidate's performance in real life versus basing their hiring decisions on resumes or interview questions.

How can one quantify hiring for character and grit? Elon Musk recently tweeted that SpaceX and Tesla both look for "a super hardcore work ethic, talent for building things, common sense and trustworthiness."[30] To add to that, he pointed out how it doesn't matter if a candidate has graduated from

---

29. Zoë Henry, "How Richard Branson Hires Remarkable People: 3 Rules," *Icons & Innovators* (blog), *Inc Magazine*, March 27, 2015.

30. Dillon Thomson, "Elon Musk Makes Surprising Tesla Recruiting Pitch: 'I Don't Care If You Even Graduated High School'," *In The Know* (blog), *Yahoo Life*, May 1, 2020.

high school or any other prior credentials. What matters most is the ability to work hard, persevere and align with the long-term vision of Tesla.

Skills can be taught through training and coaching, but character is developed through years of life experiences and cannot be easily built. One's character, mindset, and approach to dealing with situations and setbacks is a critical factor in one's career performance in the long term. Marc Benioff, the founder and CEO of Salesforce.com, built a company from the ground up based on beliefs like "Most people overestimate what they can do in the short term and underestimate what they can do in the long term." Benioff and his team at Salesforce.com are focused on long-term transformational change for the entire technology industry and to power that transformational change, Salesforce.com has focused on hiring highly driven people interested in long-term goals through their Vision, Values, Methods, Obstacles & Measures (V2MOM) methodology. V2MOM starts off with setting a longer term vision of the goals and identifies the whys behind the vision through a value based system.[31]

As outlined by the Financial Post, a study by Accenture of executives in 151 countries, concluded that the single biggest determinant of long term career success is not intelligence, educational background or experience, but rather character traits like interpersonal skills, self-awareness and social awareness.[32] People that demonstrate grit and passionately pursue long-term goals are self-aware about their struggles and the need to stay focused on the long game.

---

31. Marc Benioff, "Create Strategic Company Alignment with a V2MOM," *The 360 Blog, Salesforce.com*, May 1, 2020.
32. Ray Williams, "The Biggest Predictor of Career Success? Not Skills or Education—but Emotional Intelligence," *Financial Post*, January 1, 2014.

To better understand how leaders hire "A players" that are focused on long term goals, I spoke with Paul Greenland, VP at GMI Integrated Facility Services. Paul is a seasoned executive who has hired hundreds of people over his career. Paul's professional background is diverse and extensive. He has grown a company to fifteen hundred people spanning seven states and sold it. Most recently, he led the go-to market activities for the southwest region for a leading security and building services company.

When I first spoke to Paul about his background and career the words "My legacy is my people" struck loud and clear to me. Paul is a servant leader who is focused on helping his team grow and realizes that his success is directly attributable to his team's success and growth.

My goal in connecting with Paul was to understand how he hired and grew his teams throughout his career. What did he look for in people when hiring them? How did he hire "A players?" How did his hiring lead to scaling his businesses? Were there any lessons learned from mis-hires?

One of the most important considerations that Paul follows when hiring is grit. When I asked Paul what grit meant to him, his response was clear. Grit is the quality in an individual that represents hard work, dedication, determination, a drive that is hardwired internally and most importantly sheer willpower with an unyielding focus on the goal. Paul described grit like being a duck. Everything that is not making you get closer to your goal has to roll off your back.[33]

Paul has hired hundreds of people with grit.

---

33. Dina Gerdman, "Minorities Who 'Whiten' Job Resumes Get More Interviews," *Working Knowledge* (blog), *Harvard Business School*, May 17, 2017.

In the mid-nineties, Paul managed a large account which had a full-time onsite manager. The onsite manager was responsible for the day-to-day activities and for ensuring smooth client engagement. The onsite manager had an administrative assistant who helped with some of the administrative aspects of the job. The administrative assistant did not have a formal education and most certainly did not have a strong background in developing client relationships.

Soon after taking over the account, Paul noticed the administrative assistant was responsible for much more than the administrative aspects of the job. She had an incredible work ethic and would often be looked at by the people on the team across different shifts as the "go to" person to help with challenges. What stood out the most was that nobody had to tell the administrative assistant what to do. She identified processes and people that needed help and fixed them. In many ways, her sole focus was to ensure other people's success. After a couple of years, the onsite manager was replaced and none other than his administrative assistant took over the role of managing two hundred plus people over three shifts seven days a week.

In another example, Paul had hired an ex-marine for a sales role. The veteran did not have a formal background in sales, but he had demonstrated tremendous drive and an insurmountable appetite to learn. Over time, the new hire practiced and learned by observing his teammates and reading all the books he could find by Brian Tracy—a legendary author and speaker who trains people how to sell better and crush their sales quotas. Today, that non-traditional sales hire is Paul's top performing sales representative.

When I asked Paul how he determined someone had grit during the interview process, his response was, "Look for some adversity in their life and listen to how they handled the adversity." Adversities could be anything that deeply impacted the individual. It could be being raised in an economically disadvantaged household. It could be the divorce of parents. It could be decisions that resulted in a great deal of pain. Through adversity one develops character and character lights the fire within to work hard when no one is watching

I also inquired with Paul what were some of the reasons why new hires didn't work out. The biggest reason came down to one word: *execution*. Having the perfect resume and saying all the right things in the interview often got people hired, but when time came to actually implement the sales methodologies, what mattered most is how one converted those ideas into action. Results are based on understanding that the pursuit of the deal is in action and not words and Paul described that grit is a large component of a successful action plan.

One of Paul's most successful stories of grit was the time he pursued a prospect without much avail. He tried for years to make headway with the account, but could not get past the door. Paul came up with an ingenious plan that worked. He purchased a new pair of shoes and sent just one of the shoes in the shoe box to the prospect. In the shoebox Paul wrote, "Now that I have my foot in the door, please call me." The plan worked! Paul's grit and creative mind helped win him one of his largest accounts.

Paul's example of hiring based on work ethic and grit is similar to one used by Ranga Venkatesan.[34] Ranga is an executive at Aurea Enterprise Software and SVP of their global professional services team. When I spoke with Ranga, he

---

34. Judd B. Kesler, Corinne Low, and Colin D. Sullivan. "Incentivized Resume Rating: Eliciting Employer Preferences without Deception," *National Bureau of Economic Research* (May 2019): 4-6.

informed me that he hired stay-at-home mothers who were eager to get back to a professional work environment, but needed flexible work hours.

Ranga's experiment with hiring based on grit started when his team acquired a large enterprise software company. They needed project managers to manage large global enterprise rollouts of their product. Given how hard it was to hire project managers Ranga and his team decided to hire "outside of the mold" of the typical project manager job descriptions. Instead of looking at previous project management experience, they decided to focus on the core tasks they needed help with and at the top of that list was: *project coordination while managing multi constraints and fostering client relationships.*

Through a friend, Ranga was introduced to a stay-at-home mom who was struggling to find employment after being out of the workforce for several years. She did not have a background in project management; however, she was far more astute than most project managers given her incredible ability to manage competing priorities, set clear expectations, execute and above all, be relentless in taking care of her family and children. So, Ranga took a chance on her and looking back, he is glad he did. When I asked Ranga did if he hired her because of her skills as a mom, he replied yes. In addition, he noticed that she was "very articulate and driven to learn and grow."

At first, Ranga had his new hire shadow him and his team for three months. She observed and took notes about the daily interaction with customers. During that time, the focus was on learning through real customer engagement. After the three months, the new hire's responsibilities transitioned into managing actual customer projects and delivery. After a year, she became so good at her job that she was promoted to leader of the project management office and oversaw all new hires onboarding and training.

By taking a chance, Ranga hired someone who turned out to be an integral part of his leadership team. Her success didn't just end with training and helping others. Customers would often commend her on a job well done and would ask for her to be their project manager.

Hiring for grit and work ethic worked out really well for Aurea and their customers and it was all because a visionary leader like Ranga took a chance on someone that didn't fit the mold.

If hiring based on grit and character works for long-term success for candidates, what is the best way to identify the right character traits like grit? How can an organization find out the true character of candidates? Some organizations use personality tests. However, the main challenge with personality tests is that the questions can lead to biases. Furthermore, grading candidates based on a scale seems like just another way of judging based on a resume.

When I posted the question of measuring character and grit to Ben Gawiser, an engineering manager at Amazon, his approach was focused more on a chronological in-depth survey of one's experience and background. To use the chronological in-depth survey, an interviewer starts with the resume and asks open-ended questions about their prior experience. As the candidate responds, the interview asks detailed and open-ended, follow up questions like "What did you learn from that?" or "What were some of the mistakes you made?" These questions help identify the self-awareness and emotional intelligence of the candidate. In many ways, focus less on the actual skills related to experience and focus more on the character-building experience by leveraging situational interviewing. Ben also outlined how important it is to ask the candidate what others would say of them if asked as part of a reference check. If the responses are only focused on positive feedback, then it usually shows a lack of self-awareness. Character and grit are developed by an awareness of how others perceive us and how we can make a difference in their lives based on our sustained actions to help.

Another strategy that Ben has used to understand a candidate's character and grit is to ask them about times when they disagreed with their manager. Part of having grit has to do with having opinions and dealing with those opinions in a constructive way through persistent action by not giving up. Did the candidate accept what the manager said and just move on? Or did the candidate care enough and believe enough to prove or disprove their opinion and make a difference? Having a belief system that is derived off one's experiences and then having the courage to follow through on that belief system is a large part of having grit. That follow through becomes even more important in the face of adversity and authority. Ben outlined to me that the goal isn't to hire jerks who simply see their way as the right way. The goal is to hire people that have the ability to pursue their beliefs and have the emotional intelligence to know when they are right or when they are wrong.

In the next chapter, "Principles of Hiring for Grit", we lay the foundation and a belief system that can lead to a more effective hiring process.

PART 2

HIRE FOR GRIT FRAMEWORK

——

CHAPTER 4

PRINCIPLES OF HIRING FOR GRIT

———

By now, you must be wondering, what does "hire for grit" actually mean and how can you use it? Will hiring for grit help your organization? Should you even consider it for your organization?

We answer those questions in this and subsequent chapters.

First, let's walk through the core tenets of the *Hire for Grit* framework and the belief system that is critical to ensuring you can implement hiring for grit successfully and gain the benefits of this approach.

Hire for Grit is a recruiting framework that is based on the following four core tenets:

1. If you apply for a job, you should be given a chance to show why you are the right fit.
2. Access to information is no longer the core roadblock to learning and opportunities.
3. There are millions of "underemployed" talented people all over the world who have the potential, capability,

and grit to do much more than what they are pursuing today.

4. Hiring for character and mindset is more important in the long term than hiring for skill.

Let's review each one of the tenets in detail:

1. If you apply for a job, you should be given a chance to show why you are the right fit.

Everyone that expresses interest for a position should be given a fair and consistent chance to demonstrate they can perform the responsibilities for the role. What the candidate does with the chance to demonstrate why they are the right person for the role is up to them. The process should be a standard and consistent approach across all candidates.

In principle, this may sound like a no-brainer. Do most recruiting processes build on this belief? The short answer is no.

According to Glassdoor, a leading site for employer reviews and jobs, there are four reasons why candidates don't hear back after they apply for a role.[35] The reasons include a candidate may not be qualified, or the resume may not have the right keywords, or be formatted properly. Another common reason why candidates don't hear back is because of the sheer volume of candidates received for a position can be in the hundreds and it isn't possible to review each candidate in detail and make a determination on their fit for the role.

All the reasons that Glassdoor outlined in their blog article break this first core belief of hiring for grit. "Hire for

---

35. Meghan M. Biro, "Top 5 Reasons You Never Hear Back after Applying for a Job," *Career Advice* (blog), *Glassdoor*, February 3, 2020.

grit" means, if you apply, you should be given a chance to demonstrate why you would make a great hire. By "demonstrate", I mean you should be told more about the position by describing what types of activities you would perform if hired. You should be given a chance to show that you would be good at those responsibilities or that you have the ability to quickly learn and be productive in the role.

When everyone is given a fair and consistent chance for the role, it is not based on their resume, keywords, formatting, or factors like education and experience.

At Cloud62 we made it absolutely clear in our job postings and ads that as long as the candidate completed the recruiting case study, they were going to be called in for the interview. Going through the case study meant that the candidate invested time and energy in demonstrating their interest for the position and, hence, we were interested in learning more about them. The fact was, that most candidates didn't complete the case study and that saved us an incredible amount of time as we focused only on the candidates that demonstrated their ability to learn and deliver on the case study. Being right or wrong in the case study responses was not our concern. What mattered to us was the level of effort and logical approach a candidate took to complete what we asked them to demonstrate.

Next, let's take a look at the second belief when hiring for grit.

2. Access to information is no longer the core roadblock to learning and opportunities

The world has evolved dramatically over the last twenty years with the advent of search and social network platforms, such that, access to information and technology has made it easier for people to learn almost anything on YouTube, Udemy, Coursera and thousands of other MOOC (Massive Open Online Courses). It is no longer about access to information that determines whether you can learn, but what you do with the information that is readily available. The online education market is expected to reach $350 billion by 2025 according to Research and Market's forecasts and the accessibility of the educational content is limited only by access to the internet.[36]

People that want to learn a skill have access to limitless amounts of information, resources like videos, blogs, discussion forums and social networks for outreach.

It is important to point out that there can be a digital divide in getting access to information based on race, gender, age, income demographics and geographies, however, research has shown that the digital divide is becoming less about internet access and more about internet usage. Researchers at Washington State University and Zhejiang University have collaborated to show the reasons and outcomes of the digital divide.[37] Organizations like Cyber Security Ventures have shown that internet access is projected to triple from 2015 to 2022 when over six billion people globally will have access to information through the internet! In addition, by 2025, according to the World Advertising Research Center (WARC), 72.6 percent of internet users will access the

---

36. Renub Research, *Online Education Market & Global Forecast, by End User, Learning Mode (Self-Paced, Instructor LED), Technology, Country, Company* (United States: Renub Research, 2019).

37. Lu Wei and Douglas Hindman, "Does the Digital Divide Matter More? Comparing the Effects of New Media and Old Media Use on the Education-Based Knowledge Gap," *Mass Communication & Society* 14, no. 2 (February 2011): 216-235.

internet solely from their smart phones.[38] The world is rapidly changing and access to information and knowledge is quickly becoming universally available through smart phones.

Access to information also means people need to process and filter that information. This requires the right mindset and the discipline to learn.

One of the world's leading experts on mindset is Carol Dweck. In her bestselling book, *Mindset: The New Psychology of Success* she articulates how important a growth mindset and perseverance can be for long term success. People that have grit and a growth mindset can learn quicker and more effectively than candidates who have a fixed mindset. So, if access to information is no longer the biggest barrier to learning and growing, it boils down to the work ethic, drive, discipline, and grit to learn.

So far, we have learned that hiring for grit beliefs include giving everyone a fair and consistent chance and realizing that you can learn anything you choose using the limitless channels of information available to you. Let's take a look at the third belief and what it means to be underemployed.

3. There are millions of "underemployed" talented people all over the world who have the potential, capability, and grit to do much more than what they are pursuing today.

By "underemployed," I am referring to individuals with substantial work ethic, who have a desire for continued development; nonetheless, they struggle with pursuing a clear path for their potential. In addition to being able to live up to

---

38. Steve Morgan, "Humans on the Internet Will Triple from 2015 to 2022 and Hit 6 Billion," *Cybercrime Magazine*, July 18, 2019.

their full potential, underemployed individuals often find themselves fighting for decent full-time jobs.

According to research done by Monster.com there are over twenty-two million underemployed workers in the US who have a job that doesn't put their education, experience, or training to full use, or have no option but to work part-time when they would prefer to be working full-time.[39]

Just to be clear, underemployment is very different than unemployment. Being underemployed means you aren't fully using your strengths and skills, or you aren't challenged enough and you aren't growing in your job. Underemployed can also mean that you don't fully appreciate that the most valuable resource you have, your time, is being traded for money in working a job that doesn't bring you fulfillment. Underemployment is a systemic problem in the world we live in and there is a need to be open and mindful about it.

In addition to a non-fulfilling job, underemployed individuals would prefer full-time work with more hours; however, due to certain constraints like lack of childcare or parent care, transportation, availability, etc., they are at a disadvantage. According to the The Federal Reserve Bank of New York report on the Labor Market for Recent College Grads, over 40 percent of college graduates in the last three years didn't work at jobs that required their college degree.[40] The number of underemployed college grads has increased even more since the 2020 COVID-19 related economic recession. According to the Economic Policy Institute, one in every ten college graduates is underemployed and underemployment

39. Catherine Conlan, "Survey Finds Millions of Americans Are Underemployed," *Advice* (blog), *Monster.com*, accessed March 1, 2021.
40. Federal Reserve Bank of New York, *The Labor Market for Recent College Graduates* (New York: Federal Reserve Bank of New York, 2021).

in 2019 was greater compared to 2000 for all gender, race and ethnic groups.[41]

Finally, let's walk through the fourth belief about hiring for grit.

4. Hiring for character and mindset is more important in the long term than hiring for skill.

Skills can be learned and taught, but hard work ethic, grit, growth mindset, and other character pillars are acquired through years of life experiences, pain, failure, success and life-defining moments.

The *Hire for Grit* framework illustrates that the ability to learn, being comfortable outside your comfort zone, being curious, and accepting that failure for the pursuit of one's goals are vital character traits and a better way to hire versus looking at resumes to determine the fit for a role.

According to *Fast Company Magazine,* one of the most important factors that determine long-term career success is based on the focus on long-term goals and the sacrifices needed in the short term in pursuit of those long term goals.[42] In other words, grit is one of the most important factors that influences career trajectory.

When I interviewed David Adkins about his journey of changing tires to now being a highly successful engineering manager at Facebook, his responses all revolved around his can-do, never give up, keep trying and stay focused on the

---

41. Elise Gould, Zane Mokhiber, and Julia Wolfe, *Class of 2019: College Edition* (Washington, DC: Economic Policy Institute, 2019).

42. Tomas Chamorro-Premuzic, "True Long-Term Career Success Depends on This Most Underrated Aspect of Talent," *Fast Company* ", October 7, 2019.

long term goals. David's career success is attributed to his grit and mindset more than anything else. At Cloud62, we hired over thirty people who demonstrated grit and we prioritized character traits over skill. As a result, we were able to hire top talent and grow organically as an organization and thrive in a highly competitive environment.

It is important to note that the *Hire for Grit* approach is not intended to completely replace existing recruiting best practices. In particular, roles that require formal credentials that are gained through years of training and experience (physicians, lawyers, nuclear physicists, etc.) must still follow a strict guideline of certifications and hands-on training best practices that have been developed through years of thoughtful insight. You simply can't consider all applicants for a role of a physician as credentials and practical hands-on experience are prerequisites that cannot be ignored. You can, however, apply some of the beliefs about hiring for grit even for credentialed roles. For example, giving consideration to candidates based on their life journey and experiences and how they pursued their education and the challenges that they had to overcome can give an organization better insight about their character traits like grit.

You may have noticed that the *Hire for Grit* beliefs does not involve any personality tests or assessments to measure a 'grit score' or 'grit percentile.' I believe that the simplest way to assess someone's grit is to ask them to "Just do it." In performing tasks, you can learn a lot about an individual compared to a hypothetical generic personality test that may require some extrapolation of the results to make it applicable for the organization. Why assume that a "test" is not biased and then extrapolate the results to believe that the candidate is the right fit? Why not just better inform the candidate about the position using more than just a job description and then ask them to demonstrate how they would perform the role?

Our continued discussion in this chapter and throughout the book is based on the four core tenets. If you disagree with them or think I missed the mark, please reach out to me at hello@gritseed.com. I would love to hear your feedback and see how we can collectively make the process better.

Having reviewed the four core beliefs about hiring for grit, what can you do to get started? How can any organization improve their hiring approach to leverage the power of hiring for grit? We will review that in the next chapter.

CHAPTER 5

HIRE FOR GRIT, A SAMPLE APPROACH

———

Where should you start when hiring for grit? What are the first steps you should consider based on the four tenets we discussed previously? Let's discuss some specific examples that we have used at GRITSEED. GRITSEED is a software startup (that I founded in 2018) that has developed an automated engagement platform based on the principles of hiring for grit.

At GRITSEED, we follow a prescriptive process that is based on the *Hire for Grit* framework and empirical data collected from over one hundred thousand candidates who have applied for jobs using the *Hire for Grit* approach.

First, we start with the job description and identify ways in which we can make it more informative and inclusive. An example is removing litmus test experience requirements like the number of years of work experience. Another is to describe the day in the life of the role not based on the types of technologies and skills needed, but instead based on real work-related tasks. Leveraging the power of videos and actual employee testimonials is a great way to also inform the candidates about the role before they apply. Some of GRITSEED's customers use automated whiteboarding session videos that are an excellent way to inform candidates about working at their company. We will cover this in greater detail in subsequent chapters about how organizations can rethink their job descriptions.

Once a job description is complete, it is time to post it on job boards and channels that can lead to a diverse set of candidates applying. Instead of just posting to the same job boards that everyone else posts on, GRITSEED customers have used: billboards, bus stop ads, neighborhood and community organizations, and leveraged the power of texting over emails. According to Gartner Group, texting can result in response rates which are up to 98 percent as compared to 20 percent from emails. When organizations leverage the power of texting to connect with candidates as they apply for the role, engagement can skyrocket and can result in much wider recruiting funnels.[43] At GRITSEED, our customers typically see a dramatically more engaged recruiting process when leveraging the power of texting and videos to connect with all candidates that apply.

As you may recall, when you hire for grit, you have to ensure every candidate that applies gets a fair and consistent chance. To do that without increasing the workload on the hiring teams, an organization must use automated engagement platforms to a create a personalized experience for every candidate. This type of engagement is informative and encouraging to individuals. For example, when using

---

43. Chris Pemberton, *Tap into the Marketing Power of SMS* (Stamford, CT: Gartner, 2016).

GRITSEED, as soon as you apply, relevant questions that would typically be asked only to a selective candidate pool are asked to everyone. There is instant back and forth which is consistent across the entire candidate pool. With this approach, a recruiter doesn't typically decide who to engage with; it's engagement for everyone and the opportunity is truly democratized amongst all candidates. When posed with job simulation questions, a candidate can choose to respond or to not respond based on their interest for the role.

If you automatically give every candidate a chance to share their story and let them explain why he or she is the right fit for the role, the dependence on resumes decreases. A resume can never truly represent a candidate fully and, more importantly, a recruiter doesn't have to make any assumptions about the candidate's fit for the role by just reviewing their resume.

Organizations can also encourage candidates to finish the process using automation techniques. A common approach at GRITSEED is to send out up to three encouraging and motivational messages to candidates who have started the process, but haven't yet completed it.

To understand how the process works, assume that a company receives fifty candidates for an open position. All fifty candidates are automatically engaged and sent job simulation tasks as soon as they apply. As the candidates go through the process, recruiters have the ability to review the progress and easily extract candidates that meet certain criteria.

A recruiter can first focus on the candidates that have completed all the tasks. Next, identify candidates that actually spent one minute or more working on the tasks to weed out the ones that didn't spend a basic amount of time thinking through the tasks. Having applied two simple filters allows a recruiter to focus on a small percentage of the fifty candidates in seconds. This type of engagement can result in dramatic time savings compared to reviewing every resume.

The next step of the process is reviewing the candidate's responses for each question. That process can also be automated for certain types of tasks (e.g., multiple choice) to determine the candidate's fit. Out of the small group of candidates remaining, you can quickly run filters such as when are the candidates available to start employment or are they willing to work full time; the recruiter can filter candidates efficiently with virtually any type of question. Using automated engagement and filtering gives the recruiter an edge on focusing on the right candidates, while giving every candidate the same consistent chance.

Once the recruiter has narrowed down the list of the applicant's responses through written responses, videos, coding questions etc., they can easily be viewed and compared. These responses can eliminate the initial phone screen, which recruiters conduct to evaluate if candidates meet basic requirements. With the candidate's responses documented, the recruiter can present a standard resume and detailed notes as to why the candidate is the right fit for further interviews. This allows interviewers to focus on specific responses to the questions they have already received. Imagine seeing a coding question completed by a candidate before the candidate comes in for the in-person interview. A hiring manager can zero in on a specific part of the code and ask targeted questions about design or implementation approach created by the candidate.

This type of hiring creates a hyper-efficient process that is meaningful. If the candidate responses are not what the recruiter or hiring manager expect, one can give the candidate the option to redo a problem or choose to skip over the consideration of that candidate. The conversations with the candidate shift away from "How many years of experience do you have?" to "Please tell me why you wrote your answer this way." When reviewing a candidate for the role, all parties involved can make an informed decision about how to proceed based on the job tasks and the documented feedback.

Such an approach to hire for grit isn't just limited to applying for jobs online. It can also be used by organizations when recruiting at job fairs. The traditional process in a career fair involves waiting in a line to speak with a recruiter about the position. A recruiter can speak with hundreds of candidates at a job fair making it difficult to remember even a few. Most conversations during a job fair are the same repeated questions being posed about the work, role, culture team, etc. Leveraging videos from hiring managers, team members, and recruiters that candidates can view on their phone right when waiting in line to speak with a recruiter is an incredibly efficient way to streamline the process.

If we group the examples above, there are three key areas that need a more detailed review.

1. Rethinking Job Descriptions & Dependence on Resumes: We need to take a deeper dive into how job descriptions and resumes can result in not giving every candidate a fair chance. Also, we need to consider if job descriptions result in bias and actually narrow your recruiting funnel. Just like job descriptions, a resume may tell you in a summarized way a candidate's work experience or educational background, but there is so

much more to candidates than a piece of paper. It is hard to determine a candidate's fit for the role by just looking at a resume.

2. Use Job Simulations: Job simulations are a great way to inform candidates about the position and help them make the right decisions based on more information. Job simulations help organizations better determine if the candidate is the right fit for the role.

3. Rethinking the Role of the Recruiter: When you hire for grit, your recruiter funnel gets wider and as such you must increase your recruiting efficiency by leveraging automation and better engagement.

Before we go any further and explore the key areas, it is important to note that organizations don't have to abandon all their existing recruiting processes in favor of hiring for grit. Hiring for grit is about creating competitive talent advantages for any organization as they think about growing and succeeding in a world where talent reigns supreme.

Let's take a deeper dive into why there is an urgent need to rethink how job descriptions are used in the hiring process and why hiring for grit is a more effective approach than job descriptions and qualification checklists.

CHAPTER 6

RETHINKING JOB DESCRIPTIONS & RESUMES

Say you are the hiring manager and are actively looking to hire someone for your team. One of the first action items you will have to take on is writing a job description. Where do you start? What do you write? What does it take to write a job description that clearly outlines the roles and responsibilities and sets the right tone and expectations?

I have often struggled with these questions while recruiting for my team throughout my more than twenty year career.

Job descriptions are omnipresent in job postings and haven't evolved over the years as recruiting platforms and strategies have changed. In fact, it is extremely rare to see a job posting without an actual written job description. We live in a world of rich media—videos, pictures, games, even augmented reality, and yet, most organizations use written job descriptions that haven't advanced with the times.

Typically, a job description introduces a role, covers some highlights about the position, and then jumps right into a qualifications checklist that includes years of experience, technologies, certifications and other litmus test types of criteria that all candidates must have. Organizations often use job descriptions as a way to dissuade the *wrong* candidates from applying for the position. A perfect example of this is the "X years of experience" litmus test. It may not seem obvious at first, but job descriptions can be used as a way to reduce the workload for the parties that review applications. Another way to look at it is job descriptions can be used to limit the number of candidates going through the process and could even prevent very well-suited candidates from applying.

When implementing the *Hire for Grit* methodology, organizations have to rethink how they use job descriptions. It is time for job descriptions to receive a makeover to include a more inclusive, inviting, and engaging description of the environment. Applicants need to know what it's like to work at that organization. According to Marissa Peretz of *Forbes* magazine, the written statements in a job description can be ineffective in telling the company story, while the brand message creates a real connection with the candidate. Job descriptions are an amazing opportunity to tell an organization's and team's story.[44] You can use job descriptions to bring interested candidates to you as well as foster a way for an organization to engage with all candidates.

So what can organizations do to their job descriptions? Let's review some different strategies:

---

44. Marissa Peretz, "The Job Description Is Obsolete," *Forbes*, June 13, 2018.

Start with Culture and Values
not Job Descriptions

*"If you want to build a ship, don't drum up
the people to gather wood, divide the work,
and give orders. Instead, teach them to
yearn for the vast and endless sea."*

ANTOINE DE SAINT-EXUPÉRY, THE

AUTHOR OF *THE LITTLE PRINCE*

In 2009, Reed Hastings, the CEO of Netflix, published a deck
called "Freedom & Responsibility Culture."[45] That one hundred twenty-nine page deck was filled with the secret sauce
that has made Netflix immensely successful. The "Freedom
& Responsibility Culture" consists of who gets hired at Netflix and who gets to remain at Netflix. That deck goes away
from "nice-sounding" value statements to truths that matter
to Netflix and how Netflix hires, rewards, promotes, and
values their team.

Organizations should create a list of values that are based
on their *why*—why they exist, what they stand for, and how
decisions will be made. When there is a fork in the road,
the path forward is often determined by the values system.
Hence, for any organizations, their values are the core of
what defines them. If hiring the right people is one of the

---

45. Reed Hastings, "Freedom and Responsibility Culture" (Slideshare presentation, online at Slideshare.com, 2009).

most important decisions an organization can make, it is critical to make that decision in alignment with the values that define the organization and its culture.

Organizations must put their values first when hiring people. The values and culture must be clearly defined first in the hiring process. Organizations should make it less about litmus tests and years of experience and more about demonstrating why a candidate is the right fit based on values and culture.

Is the candidate in line with the organization's values?

Which values can they most relate to?

Can a candidate demonstrate from their past experience or education how they aligned with the organization's values?

Will the candidate fit in to the corporate culture that is defined by the values?

These are some of the questions that an organization must answer. For Netflix, independent decision making, sharing information, being candid, retaining highly effective people, and avoiding rules are the values that they care about most. Those values are all over Netflix's careers page and a critical part of the evaluation and hiring process that is followed.[46]

---

46. "Netflix Jobs," Netflix, accessed February 28, 2021.

Make Job Descriptions Inclusive
& Gender Neutral

According to research published in the Journal of Personality and Social Psychology in 2011, job ads for male dominated occupations used masculine words more frequently than feminine words.[47] The research also shows that job ads that used more masculine words affected perceptions of gender diversity, job appeal, and fitting in *not* based on personal ability.

In 2014, the *Harvard Business Review* published an article stating "Men apply for a job when they meet only 60 percent of the qualifications, but women apply only if they meet 100 percent of them."[48] Based on these findings, the reasons women don't apply can be summarized in two ways:

1. Believing that one is qualified for the job is important
2. It is considered respectful to follow the guidelines set forth in the job description

As such, the perception that a job description creates is not gender independent. So, what can organizations do to address these important findings?

First, organizations can make their job descriptions gender neutral by being mindful of the reasons why one gender may choose not to apply for a position. Organizations can use gender neutral words throughout the job description, as this encourages both men and women to apply for the role.

---

47. Danielle Gaucher et. al., "Evidence That Gendered Wording in Job Advertisements Exists and Sustains Gender Inequality," *Journal of Personality and Social Psychology* 101, no. 1 (January 2011): 109-128.
48. Tara Sophia Mohr, "Why Women Don't Apply for Jobs Unless They're 100% Qualified," *Harvard Business Review*, August 25, 2014.

As noted in the research paper by Danielle Gaucher, Justin Friesen and Aaron Kay, some examples of gender specific words that you should try to be aware of when using in a job description are[49]:

List of Masculine and Feminine Words
Coded in Studies 1 and 2[50]

Masculine-coded words	Feminine-coded words
active	agree
adventurous	affectionate
aggress	child
ambition	cheer
analyze	collab
assert	commit
athletic	communal
autonomous	compassion
battle	connect
boast	considerate
challenge	cooperate
champion	co-operate
compete	depend
confident	emotional
courage	empathy
decide	feel
decision	flatterable
decisive	gentle
defend	honest
determine	interpersonal
	interdependent
dominant	interpersonal

---

49. Kat Matfield, "Gender Decoder for Job Ads," Gender Decoder, November 5, 2018.
50. Ibid.

Masculine-coded words	Feminine-coded words
driven	inter-personal
fearless	inter-dependent
fight	inter-personal
force	kind
greedy	kinship
head-strong	loyal
headstrong	modesty
hierarch	nag
hostile	nurture
impulsive	pleasant
independent	polite
individual	quiet
intellect	responsive
lead	sensitive
logic	submissive
objective	support
opinion	sympathy
outspoken	tender
persist	together
principle	trust
reckless	understand
self-confident	warm
self-reliant	whiny
self-sufficient	enthusiastic
self-confident	inclusive
self-reliant	yield
self-sufficient	share
stubborn	sharing
superior	
unreasonable	

Using gender neutral job descriptions and ads are especially important for occupations where one gender is more common than the other. According to *ISE Magazine*, women only make up 25 percent of the technology roles as compared to 75 percent of males even though women make up over half the US workforce.[51] Why is that? It may boil down to engaging females at an early age in learning skills that are needed to become a programmer, but also from removing the biases that exist in the talent acquisition process. Organizations must create environments that reward each gender equally and that has to start with how talent gets acquired in the first place. A great first step in removing the biases is to be mindful of how a job is represented in the job description. Secondly, those involved in the hiring process need to be aware of how a job description can turn people away from applying.

The goal of a job description should be to encourage as many candidates to apply and yet, it is often used as a weeding-out mechanism by consciously (or subconsciously) discouraging people from applying.

Reduce Litmus Test and Checklist based Requirements

Most job descriptions have requirements that say "X years of experience" or "must have a college degree." Organizations use these types of litmus test requirements for several reasons. The most obvious is the extrapolation that years of experience and an educational background will translate into someone

---

51. Human Network Contributor, "The Latest Stats on Women in Tech," *ICT Solutions & Education*, October 1, 2020.

automatically being qualified for the position. Assume for a minute that there is a direct and consistent correlation between years of experience/educational background and performance on the job. But is there a better way to determine if someone is qualified for the role? Is there a way that doesn't leverage the assumption that years of experience and educational background will indeed translate into finding someone that will be a highly productive member of the team and the *best* person for the role?

Here are some questions to consider when writing the requirements part of job descriptions:

- How do you know what the X in "X years of work experience" should be? Do numbers like three or five or ten have a direct meaning or correlation to job performance? Is there a way *not* to use years of experience as a litmus test?
- How do you really know if three years of experience is not enough when you use a five-year experience requirement?
- How can the actual quality of those years of experience be measured? A candidate with five years of experience in a role that doesn't challenge them may not be as effective as someone with two years of highly challenging experience.
- What about education requirements? If someone doesn't have a master's degree, does that truly matter for the role?
- How much of what you learned in college did you use in your first job and continue to use today? Based on that, is it fair to expect all candidates to have college degrees?
- If the education requirements are used to demonstrate commitment to one's goals, are there other life experiences and choices that can demonstrate the same?

These are hard questions that have no black and white answers. These questions should inspire organizations to think of creative ways to determine, with a reasonable level of certainty, the candidate they choose is the right candidate based on empirical data and not extrapolated checklist requirements like experience and education.

Don't get me wrong. Hiring for grit doesn't mean you should not use any educational or experience requirements. I am merely saying don't make them gatekeeper requirements. Focus more on letting a candidate show you why they are the right fit for the role versus making a judgment call based on a checklist.

The good news is companies, especially technology, manufacturing oriented companies are making job requirements less about educational backgrounds. Companies like Apple hired nearly 50 percent of their recruits in 2018 who didn't have a formal four-year college education.[52] Lockheed Martin hired fourteen thousand people in 2018 that didn't have a formal four-year education.[53] IBM is another example of an organization that has deviated from a formal four-year degree requirement to hire entry-level talent.

Use Videos to Show and Engage Candidates

Are written job descriptions really the best way to describe the job duties of a position? We live in a world dominated by video content. We are rapidly moving towards 5G networks

---

52. Mikey Campbell, "Half of New Apple's US Hires in 2018 Lacked 4-Year College Degrees, Cook Says," *Apple Insider* (blog), 2020.

53. David Shepardson, "CEOs Tell Trump They Are Hiring More Americans without College Degrees," Aerospace & Defense, *Reuters*, March 6, 2019.

with even more bandwidth and power to deliver high quality content. Organizations should leverage the power of video for several reasons. First, video is easier to consume and digest. Imagine how the old adage "A picture is worth a thousand words" would be translated in the world of videos? "A one-minute video is worth a million words?"

Many organizations already use the power of videos to better engage with candidates by showcasing their mission and culture. Nonetheless, can organizations do more with video? Is showing videos on a careers page enough?

Several strategies to leverage videos come to mind when you make a commitment to hire for grit.

First, you have to use videos as a cornerstone for the entire process and not just as a "one size fits all" generic marketing video on the careers page. You have to create videos for each step of the process. It is important to note that you don't have to leverage many resources or have a big budget to create videos. You can simply use 'selfie' style videos created on a cellphone. Those types of videos can be used to connect with candidates in a much more authentic way than professionally produced videos. The goal is not to impress using sophisticated editing and production. The goal of the *Hire for Grit* videos is to demonstrate and to educate every candidate about the actual position and what they would experience and how it would feel to be on the job. This way, the candidate can make an informed decision about the position. Organizations should use the power of videos to encourage candidates to apply and to also present themselves as supportive and inclusive of all.

Here are some examples of videos that an organization can create for each position:

- Show a day in the life of the role. Walk candidates through the day in the life. Show your manufacturing floor, show your retail location, show your workspace, show your call center environment, show your territory commute and a sample prospect meeting.
- Provide the opportunity for the hiring manager and peers to share their experiences of working on a team.
- Create videos where a hiring manager white boards real examples of challenges they solve every day.
- Share core beliefs through the eyes of the executives—their why, the organization's story, mission, and belief system. This can be hugely powerful for any candidate that is aligned with the core mission.
- Leverage videos that describe the training that a candidate would go through once hired.
- Exhibit videos that demonstrate real job situations such as a customer calling in with a complaint.
- Utilize videos to thank candidates for going through the application process. It is a great way for organizations to better connect with talent versus the standard "We will get back to you in seven to ten business days" email.
- Produce videos that inform candidates of the application process and also encourage them to complete it.

Be creative with your job descriptions

Job descriptions are a great way to tell your organization's and team's unique story. Job descriptions present an opportunity to make an impression with active and passive candidates. Be sure to make a distinct impression that will encourage all candidates to apply.

For example, it is common for a job description to use the phrase "You should have excellent communication skills and the ability to work well with customers to resolve their complaints."

The job description for the same job could be described this way: "Customers will call you with issues or complaints about our product. You will be empowered to help them address billing issues by thinking outside the box and converting every upset customer into a delighted customer."

Remember to leverage your marketing team when creating a job description. Don't simply copy, paste, and tweak a similar role's job description that you found online or on other job boards. Ask yourself if the *job description creates a compelling story and call to action* for every candidate to apply.

Lastly, evaluate the job description's performance. How many candidates clicked on the job description versus how many applied? Out of the ones that applied, how many completed the process? Be sure to include videos of hiring managers and team peers directly on the application page—before a candidate even applies. A company can use this type of engagement strategy to convert candidates who may not have applied for the position. Have frank conversations with your candidates over videos. If your organization is struggling to hire more women for tech roles, be open about it and specifically encourage females to apply by sharing success stories of previous female hires.

Reduce dependence on resumes

Resumes are at the core of all recruiting applications and processes.

Resumes quickly tell you more about a candidate, their work history, educational background, accomplishments, skills etc. Sometimes organizations also look at how the resume is represented, the formatting, spelling mistakes or grammatical errors, and other representations that may give some additional indications about the candidate. In recent years, companies have automatically scanned resumes and extrapolated the "best ones" using algorithms and rankings.

When a candidate applies, they are typically required to submit a resume. Resumes are used by recruiters and hiring managers to evaluate the "fit" for the role. Resumes are often the first and only way for a candidate to tell their story and to convince a recruiter or hiring manager to move forward to the next phase of the hiring process. Cover letters can sometimes be used, but the fact of the matter is, when you have tens or hundreds of applicants for a position, it can be time pressing to read every cover letter. Thus, quickly reviewing a resume is the only option. In many cases a resume is the only tool used in determining a candidate's chance to progress to the next round of the process—and that determination can sometimes be made in seconds or minutes.

So, what is wrong with using resumes?

For starters, candidates and recruiters often play the 'keyword game.' Given the limited resources and time to review all applications for a position, a recruiter may be forced to quickly scan for keywords across all resumes received for the position. Candidates are well aware of that strategy and often create a resume packed with keywords that increases the chances of their resume showing up on the recruiter's radar. This approach to zeroing in on the right candidate is fundamentally flawed, but what other options are there for recruiters to find the right candidates? There are clear, less biased ways of using job simulations, which we will discuss later in this chapter.

The larger question is: Does a resume really represent a candidate? Just like a traditional job description can't fully represent and describe what it is like to work at a company, resumes present a one-dimensional and poor view of a candidate. Not only are resumes difficult for organizations to make an informed decision about the candidate, but they also prove too difficult for candidates to properly demonstrate and explain why they would be an asset in that given role.

As we mentioned earlier, resumes can lead to conscious or unconscious biases. By removing references to names, gender, and other identifiable information, we can give every candidate an equal chance. When it is time to reveal the candidate's name and other identifiable information, human resources professionals should create an audit trail to ensure compliance of any bias concerns.

We have seen how organizations can use job descriptions to widen the recruiting funnel when hiring for grit. We have also learned how resumes can lead to biases and discussed what organizations can do to proactively address those biases.

But, what else can be done when hiring for grit? That's the focus of our next chapter.

CHAPTER 7

USING JOB SIMULATIONS BEFORE HIRING

———

Have you hired someone only to realize it was the wrong decision? What if there was a way to reduce the likelihood of making a wrong hiring decision? Have you started a job just to realize it wasn't for you? Is there a way to be more confident about your decision before you embark on a new job opportunity?

Job simulations can help organizations make more informed hiring decisions while simultaneously providing a superior method to making career decisions for candidates.

Think of job simulations as a mini clip into the typical workday. It can be a robust tool to showcase your environment while educating job applicants. This provides an informative approach with real problems, challenges, and job duties rather than the standard job description. Organizations have the freedom to create job specific tasks that align with all positions. Imagine sending a customized simulation, leveraging videos, and actual job duty representations to candidates as they apply.

When you hire for grit, job simulations should be used early on in the application process as possible and must be given to **all** candidates that apply. If everyone is given the same chance, the process remains consistent, fair and any biases introduced based on criteria like their resume, keywords, and experience can be kept in check. As soon as a candidate applies, they should be presented with videos and tasks that they can complete *at their own time where they can start and stop as they choose.* The sooner you engage with candidates the better and it is vital to make the experience totally seamless regardless of device and location.

You may be questioning if candidates actually engage that early on in the process and perform the job simulations. The short answer is *yes.* Candidates that are genuinely interested in the position watch the videos to learn more about the role and if they still have interest, will go through the process. GRITSEED is a recruiting automation platform that follows the *Hire for Grit* blueprint and allows organizations to present job simulations to all candidates. Empirical results from over one hundred thousand candidates that used GRITSEED clearly show that most candidates prefer this type of engagement. If they are truly interested, they actively answer questions and perform the tasks presented to them.

I have worked with many different types of organizations and helped them hire hundreds of people using the power of job simulations. Some of the examples include roofers, manufacturing line workers, carpenters, hospitality staff that became software developers. Others include bartenders who became great salespeople. The list goes on. By using job simulations, organizations were able to find incredible talent that they wouldn't have considered otherwise.

Institutions can use job simulations in varying ways based on the actual role. For roles that have a serious talent shortage (narrow recruiting funnel), you should consider fewer tasks for the job simulation. Even consider opportunities to create more content as part of the simulation to "sell" your organization to the candidates. For roles which have very wide recruiting funnels on the top (in other words, an abundance of talent) you should leverage more job tasks to zero-in on the right candidates.

When I spoke to Farhan Thawar, VP of Engineering at Shopify, about his approach to hiring the best talent, the answer was unequivocal.

"The best way to know if a candidate is the right fit for the role is not to judge them using their resume or even interview them. The best way to know is to actually give them on-the-job tasks."

Farhan's approach to reducing bias has been to reduce the time he and his team spend with candidates when interviewing them (they have it down to an art of just fifteen-minute interviews for some of the technical roles). Farhan and his team spend time with candidates "in-role" vs. "in-interview" and that approach has helped them hire incredible people who empirically show that they are the right fit for the position.

There are several benefits of using job simulations. They include:

1. Increasing Diversity & Widening the Recruiting Funnel

Job simulations help you see how a candidate would perform since they are performing the tasks. So long as the simulations are given to all candidates that apply, you increase the likelihood of considering candidates that you may not have considered otherwise.

2. Saving Time & Money

An organization can save time using a fully automated simulation system with everyone assigned the same tasks automatically. More importantly, the recruiter and the hiring manager can see how the candidate did versus the traditional process of looking at a candidate's resume or 'fit' for the role. Instead of a hiring manager or recruiter deciding which candidates to select for the next step of the process, the candidate removes themselves from the process by not completing the assigned tasks. A candidate may choose not to continue the process if they believe the role is not a good fit for them. Ultimately, the organization can avoid wasting time, money and the potential heartache of the wrong hire.

3. Reducing Employee Attrition

When hiring mangers provide information about the tasks, candidates can make informed decisions. At GRITSEED, we have seen empirical data that shows that making informed decisions about career opportunities results in reduced attrition rates of up to 25 percent.

Okay, so job simulations may be the least widely used and best kept secret when recruiting talent, but how can it be used for specific positions?

Let's look at some real examples.

The Sales Development Representative (SDR) role is a very common position that companies are constantly hiring for. There are over fifty-eight thousand open jobs in early 2021 for that role across America as shown on Indeed![54] That's a lot of opportunity for people looking for a career in sales. What types of job simulations can organizations use when hiring SDRs?

Sales Role Job Simulation Ideas

Type of Simulation	Task	Notes
Simple Write-up	Tell us what separates a really good salesperson from an average salesperson.	The goal is to see if the candidate understands that if you want to excel at sales, you have to help people and build trust/ relationships first.
Prospecting Ability	Assume the territory that will be assigned to you is Western NY. Do research on our company and identify three prospect/leads that could be interested in what we offer.	Great way to see if the candidate understands what the organization actually does and how to value sell to prospects

54. "Sales Development Representative," Search Results, Indeed, accessed January 22, 2021.

Type of Simulation	Task	Notes
Communication Style	Write an introductory email introducing yourself and company.	Does the candidate write long "sales" emails or is the candidate focused on helping the prospect?
Video	Create a short video introducing yourself during the first meeting with one of the prospects.	See how the candidate represents themselves in a meeting? What is their energy like?
Follow-up	Send a follow-up note to a prospect and leave a thirty second voicemail.	Critical for salespeople to follow up and keep the sales cycle going. How do they communicate in the follow up?
Closing Deals	How would you close this deal? What are some impediments that you could anticipate and proactively handle?	Does the candidate have the "art of the close"?

The questions and tasks above focus on the typical day-to-day functions of an SDR. If a candidate is able to respond to the questions and task with answers that are thoughtful and clearly demonstrate their ability to perform the jobs and duties of an SDR, then regardless of their background or experience, they should be considered for an in-person interview. Using the approach above, the initial step of determining whether the candidate is qualified or if they should be considered is no longer based on a person's resume, but rather based on the candidate's demonstration of their fit for the role.

At GRITSEED, we have noticed that there is a positive correlation and outcome in hiring SDR people who have worked as bartenders, country club staff, sports team members, and many others. This type of interdisciplinary transfer of job skills also allows organizations to think outside the box and widen the recruiting funnel.

Similar to SDR roles, there are over three hundred thousand jobs on Indeed (as of early 2021) that are related to the development of software.[55] We have repeatedly heard from industry leaders like Microsoft, Google, and Apple to name a few, that there just aren't enough technically skilled people available in the United States to meet the needs of the industry. In a recent blog article about Internet of Things (IoT), Microsoft Sr. Director of IoT Marketing, made the case that over 47 percent of companies looking to hire technical talent are not able to do so because of the shortage of talent.[56]

What can organizations do to fill the technical talent shortage? At Cloud62, my first startup, I was faced with a similar dilemma. I had to hire technical talent that was proficient in Salesforce.com yet I simply couldn't find that talent in the Western New York area, so I decided to use the *Hire for Grit* framework and hire people who had grit with a growth-oriented mindset and an analytical background, regardless of technical education. To find these unique individuals, I used a series of analytical tasks. People that went through the process demonstrated to me and my team that they were capable of learning and becoming technical experts. The candidates that chose not to complete the process were often glad that they were able to make an informed decision about the role before they got hired; they were happier pursuing opportunities that interested them more.

55. "Software Engineer, Entry-Level," Search Results, Indeed, accessed January 22, 2021.
56. Jaishree Subramania, "Addressing the Coming IoT Talent Shortage," *Microsoft Industry Blogs*, Microsoft, September 16, 2019.

Entry Level Technology Role Job Simulation Ideas

Type of Task	Task	Notes
Analytical	Solve a brain teaser or a constraint satisfaction problem or even a Sudoku puzzle!	The goal is to see if the candidate goes through and answers the question based on a logical thought process. Does the candidate have the patience that will be needed in the role?
Online Research to Solve Problems	Show some facts and fiction and ask the candidate to perform Google searches to determine what is fact and what is fiction.	Most technical people spend an incredible amount of time researching solutions to problems and browsing sites like Stackoverflow. Will the candidate have the ability to do the same and learn?
Ability to Self-Learn and Communicate	Read a dense documentation guide or tutorial and ask the candidate to summarize what they learned.	Can the candidate read through technical documentation, understand and communicate what they learned?
Code	Write code for a simple problem. E.g., Write a simple application in the language of your choice (or choose Python) that prints a list of prime numbers between two numbers.	Observe how the code was written for consistency in formatting, variable names, method names and ensure it was indeed run with results.
Communication Skills	Create a short video talking about what you developed in the last task talk (Include what you developed, any challenges you faced and anything your team member should know.)	Great way to see if the candidate actually wrote the code! Also, assess communication style and skills.

We have seen examples of very specific sales and technical roles; however, can this same type of hiring approach be applied to a more generic role like a customer service rep?

The short answer is yes. One of GRITSEED's customers, Capital Management Services, has hired hundreds of people this way. Similar to the sales and technical job simulation ideas, organizations can leverage customer service-oriented simulations to get a better idea of non-tangible skills that a candidate would bring to the role.

Customer Service Role Job Simulation Ideas

Type of Task	Task	Notes
Customer Scenario	Use the provided call script and demonstrate how you would deal with the customer situation. Write your response or use video.	Can the candidate follow a call script that they will have to use every day? Can they improvise?
Judgment Call and Situational Awareness	Play a sample call and ask how the customer service agent handled the call and what they did correctly and where they could have done better	There is no right or wrong answer here. The goal is to keep it open-ended for a candidate to understand situational awareness.
Think Outside the Box	Ask the candidate to think how to create WOW experiences for a customer. How can you convert an upset customer into a delighted customer for life?	Using specific examples of situations, you can quickly determine a candidates ability to think "outside the job description."
Proactive-ness	Can a candidate identify situations that could lead to customer attrition if not handled appropriately?	Another example of thinking "outside the job description."

The above examples are just a small sample of the job tasks that could be presented to the candidates.

A big question that you may have is how you determine what job simulations and tasks to present. The easiest way to determine what to present to every candidate is by asking a hiring manager or a top performer on the hiring team to come up with a list of questions that are important to the role. Job simulations should represent the daily actions that are taken to perform the job. It is less about asking questions that measure skill and more about questions that will ensure the person will be able to perform effectively in the role. You should also carefully craft the wording of the questions you post. Don't ask questions like "How many years of work experience do you have as a product manager?" Rather, ask questions like "Tell us about a product that you have used, designed or managed. What are some of the important constraints you had to deal with? How was the product developed? What did the team look like?"

According to Farhan Thawar, VP of Engineering at Shopify, interviewing and hiring based on someone's resume or experience doesn't mean that the candidate is likely to be a high performer.[57] The best way to know if someone will actually be good is to "let them drive." Let them show you what they can do not under a simulated test or a whiteboarding session but rather through actual performance of job-related tasks. Farhan argues that organizations should actually take it one step further and hire people on probation for the first ninety days and determine the fit for the role based on actual job performance.

Farhan also points out that technical interviews can lead to a biased experience for the disadvantaged who are often

---

57. Farhan Thawar, "Technical Interviews Are Garbage. Here's What We Do Instead," *Medium* (blog), October 20, 2017.

given tasks under high pressure situations and expected to perform flawlessly. The fact is top technical performers are the ones that are resourceful and have grit and there is very little correlation between someone interviewing well and actually performing well on the job. In fact, there are those that perform poorly on interviews, yet do exceptionally well if given the opportunity. According to Gayle Laakmann McDowell, Ex-Googler, Author of *Cracking the Coding Interview* and *The Google Resume*, a study at Google found that interview performance had no correlation to job performance.[58]

When I started GRITSEED, I was determined to use job simulations to find good software developers that may not appear to be a good fit on paper. That's when I first met Jesse. Jesse was nervous and didn't interview that well. Nevertheless, Jesse was given a set of tasks to demonstrate what he could do and how he would write code. Jesse showed real commitment by learning what he didn't know.

It is important to note that the simulations can embrace a *growth mindset* approach. When presenting candidates with job tasks, you should be open and give candidates a chance to show you they can learn quickly based on their transferrable skills. You can clearly state that a candidate may not have any experience for what you are looking for and that is okay.

You may not have any experience with product management, but that's okay.

Think of a product that you love to use. What do you think makes the product great?

---

58. Gayle Laakmann, "Is There a Link between Job Interview Performance and Job Performance?," *Forbes*, June 28, 2013.

If you were the product manager of the product, what would you do differently?

We have seen how job simulations can be used as part of the hiring process to give everyone a chance and to help all parties make informed decisions that are based less on assumptions and more about actual data.

Next, let's review some of the benefits of using the *Hire for Grit* framework and how any organization can find value by adopting the approaches we have discussed.

CHAPTER 8

RETHINKING THE RECRUITER'S ROLE

What is the most important asset for any organization? If you ask that question to most executives, the answer will be unequivocally: people are the most important asset. According to Peter Drucker, one of the most respected management researchers and educators:

> "The most valuable asset of a twenty-first century institution, whether business or non-business, will be its knowledge, workers, and their productivity."

If people are an organization's greatest asset, then a recruiter who is responsible for recruiting the right people has a very important role for the organization's long-term success. However, recruiters have a hard job in pursuing talent while keeping in mind time and budget considerations. Not to mention the same talent is often sought after by the competition.

Recruiters often work directly with hiring managers before starting the search. A hiring manager's expectations and hopes depend on a recruiter finding the right person, at the right time, within the compensation constraints and convince that candidate to join the organization. Wow! Those types of expectations can lead to an incredible amount of pressure and stress for any recruiter.

To better understand how hard a recruiter's job can be, let's take an example. Say you are a recruiter and tasked to scout out and recruit players for a football team. Assume you have a general understanding of football and enjoy watching the sport, but haven't really been involved in recruiting football players even though you have recruited soccer players in the past. Assume you have a high-level idea of each type of player, role, and know who the great players are yet haven't really seen what the great players do behind the scenes when they are not playing games.

How would you go about recruiting players for the team? Would you start with physical characteristics like height or weight? Would you consider how fast a player can run? Or how they can tackle others? Would you look at their past performance in games? Those would be all good places to start, but, what else could you do?

When you hire for grit, you should consider spending time embedding yourself within your team. You should consider attending every practice and coaching sessions, listening to what the players and coaches talk about every day. You should consider how the players play as a team and try to identify where the gaps are. You should understand the personalities of the existing team players and identify what types of players may be a great fit given the existing dynamics of the team. You must get to know the game of football well so you can make informed decisions about candidates that are based on real experiences and not assumptions based on your limited knowledge of the game. A candidate who may look great based on their past performance may not work out so great for the team you are recruiting for. Everyone has strengths and weakness. Your role as a recruiter should compare the strengths of a candidate versus the needs of a team and the gaps that exist while considering the interpersonal dynamics of the team.

I used the example of recruiting for a football team because everyone understands the importance of working together as a team to become champions. The same type of logic and approach applies to high performing teams in the corporate world.

You may ask, how can one spend time with the actual teams and understand the dynamics when hiring managers are already drowning in resumes, meetings and coordination activities? Recruiters are already swamped with so much to do, how can we expect them to add more to their plate?

According to Recruiter.com, recruiters spend over 63 percent of their time every week on the phone speaking with candidates.[59] In addition, recruiters also spend an incredible amount of time reviewing resumes and past experiences across a large candidate pool. The pool of candidates that a recruiter spends time with is incredibly large and is analogous to casting a wide net, then meeting with and reviewing as many candidates as possible to find the right one. Is that the most efficient use of time?

When an organization decides to hire for grit, a recruiter focuses less on looking at resumes or the number of years of work experience. A recruiter spends less time with outreach

---

59. Fernando Ramirez, "5 Compelling Statistics about Recruiting Behavior," *Recruiting* (blog), *Recruiter.com*, September 16, 2014.

to prospective candidates trying to convince them to apply. Hiring for grit means that instead of focusing on as many candidates as possible to find the one right candidate, you let the right candidate(s) come to you. It is about reducing the workload on a recruiter and not increasing by orders of magnitude. Hiring for grit is about focusing on the right tasks by working smart not hard.

So how can we reimagine the role of a recruiter when hiring for grit? There are five *Hire for Grit* strategies that can help any recruiter save time, focus on the right candidates, and help hire incredible talent:

Focus on widening the recruiting funnel NOT narrowing it.

One of the most important roles of a recruiter is to get as many people to apply for the position as possible. The more people that apply, the higher the chance of finding the best and most suited candidate. A recruiter should move past litmus test requirements that are used in job descriptions to limit the candidate pool and instead focus on making the job description inclusive and qualifications as encouraging as possible.

A recruiter should not be focused on reviewing every candidate's background and resume. By letting the *Hire for Grit* framework take charge, the recruiter focuses only on the candidates that complete the job simulations. If you recall, job simulations provide a great tool to communicate to all candidates what it is like to work in that particular role. The purpose of those simulations is to help the candidate make an informed decision about their interest in the role. An important assumption here is that only the candidates that are truly interested in the role will go through the extensive exercise of the simulation.

If the candidate pool is expected to be extremely large, then a recruiter can create longer simulations and tasks to see which candidates are the most committed and interested. This type of selection process must be consistent, fair, and about democratizing the opportunity for all.

Instead of searching for candidates, focus on telling authentic stories about your company, culture, values, team, and be humble about areas of improvement.

In addition to job descriptions, a recruiter should leverage the power of videos to tell the company, team and role story. By videos, I don't mean generic marketing videos or videos that show the perks of working for the company. An organization should focus on authentic videos that are filled with true stories, of real individuals, and the good and the bad of working at the organization.

By being authentic in the story and role description, an organization leads by example for all the candidates to learn about the company culture and values. Authenticity in the stories about the role also drives diversity in the candidate pool as candidates see and realize that there is no such thing as the perfect job and it's okay for them to represent themselves as imperfect yet a good fit for the role.

A recruiter should consider themselves as the creative and video director of telling the company and team story.

Give every candidate a fair and consistent chance by letting them demonstrate.

A recruiter should take themselves out of the initial review process to determine who gets a chance or moves to the next step in the process. By default, every candidate that applies using the *Hire for Grit* framework gets a chance. By reducing the need to review all the resumes and candidates, a recruiter can save an incredible amount of time.

At GRITSEED, my startup focused on the *Hire for Grit* framework, our customers say the biggest benefit is the time savings in seeking out the right candidate. Customers will often tell us that by using automation and giving everyone the same opportunity, there are results in focusing on candidates who may not only be a good fit for the role, but are deeply committed and interested.

Don't make assumptions about a candidate's fit for the role. Rely on job simulation data and results, not assumptions.

A recruiter must try hard not to make assumptions about a candidate's fit for the role based on keywords or what's found on a resume. Rather, a recruiter should rely on hard data that can be easily seen in a candidate's attempt to complete the simulations presented to them. Data points like their responses to the questions, their time spent on the simulations, the questions they asked about the simulation, the creativity in responding and many other attributes that can be reviewed by a recruiter as well as the hiring team.

A recruiter should strictly avoid presenting a subset of the candidates to the hiring team based on just looking at a resume. The hiring team should make an attempt to look at all the candidates that put in the time and effort to complete the simulations and counter the candidate's time and commitment with their own by giving them fair consideration.

Focus on candidates who want the job more than anyone else. Balance a candidate's existing skills and ability to learn for the needs of the job.

As we discussed earlier, the role of a recruiter is to find the right person who is truly interested and committed to the role, and someone who has the ability to execute if hired. The right candidate should be someone who has the abilities and people skills to work well on the team. That could be someone with years of relevant experience or even someone without the experience but who has the ability to learn quickly and be a hyper-productive member of the team.

In the first chapter, we discussed how hiring for character is more important in the long term than hiring just based on skills and experience. The right people with the right attitude can shape the future and progress of an entire team and using the *Hire for Grit* framework you will encounter people that you may not have considered otherwise. A recruiter's focus should be on people that demonstrate commitment, capabilities, and the ability to persevere.

In this chapter, we have reviewed how hiring for grit saves a recruiter an incredible amount of time and energy from having to review resumes and keywords and from focusing on a very large candidate pool. Hiring for grit can save any recruiter time and allow them to focus on tasks that can create a meaningful difference in hiring the most valued asset for any organization.

PART 3

HIRE FOR GRIT CONSIDERATIONS

—

CHAPTER 9

BENEFITS OF HIRING FOR GRIT

––––––

We have looked at what it means to hire for grit and how an organization can go about hiring that way. But why is hiring for grit important? What are some of the benefits of hiring this way? Is there a real need to change how hiring is done? The short answer is, YES!

There is an urgent need to consider other hiring frameworks instead of relying on existing processes, but using the *Hire for Grit* framework produces a myriad of benefits.

Benefit: Hire for Grit Reduces Bias and Increases Diversity

There are several ways in which conscious or unconscious bias is reduced and diversity is increased when you hire for grit.

When organizations write their job descriptions in a gender-neutral way, encouraging more candidates to apply versus using checklists for qualifications can make an impactful difference in reducing bias and increasing diversity. In Chapter Six, we reviewed several strategies on how to better write job descriptions and the type of language to use. Next, when you hire for grit, every candidate that applies for the position is given a chance. If you recall in Chapter Four, one of the core tenets of hiring for grit is giving every candidate that applies a fair and consistent chance. The proper approach is having every candidate demonstrate how they represent the core beliefs of the organization. This approach greatly reduces biases that may arise by only reviewing a resume.

Don't get me wrong. I am aware and understand the importance of experience and education but at the same time, it is important to know that by looking at just experience and education it may result in bias and you may miss out on a candidate who could be an amazing fit given their transferrable skills, mindset, ability to learn, and grit. If I had let my bias get in the way of giving Pete Lyons a chance, would Pete have been where he is today? Would he have become a Salesforce.com MVP helping others learn and grow their careers?

When I spoke to Glenn Jackson, the Chief Diversity Officer at M&T Bank about strategies of increasing diversity and inclusion for any organization, his response was clear: organizations that give everyone a chance to demonstrate their fit for the role directly contribute to the democratization of opportunity. Hiring for grit is exactly that. Reduce bias and increase inclusion by democratizing opportunity for all.

Videos are a big part of the *Hire for Grit* process. But can videos increase bias and reduce diversity? There are two types of videos that an organization can leverage: recruiting videos describing the company, people, culture, and role *and* candidate video uploads as requested by the organization.

An organization's recruiting videos can be tremendously helpful and tell a much better story about the role, team and work environment than a job description can. Every organization has to be mindful that the videos they create are good representations of the team and promote authenticity. When you encourage team members to be authentic, you allow diversity to flourish. If organizations produce videos with those principles in mind, candidates are encouraged and it can help reduce bias in the process and increase diversity.

Can an organization asking candidates to create videos lead to race, age or other types of biases? The short answer is yes, *but* the bias that arises from candidate videos is no less than any bias that can result during in-person interviews.

In 2010 the Equal Employment Opportunity Commission (EEOC) released an informal letter that talks about video interviews.[60] In those bulletins they stated as long as employers keep appropriate records of all applicants, create a standardized process across all applicants, complied with Equal Employment Opportunity (EEO) laws and implemented proactive measures to minimize risk of discrimination and leveraged best practices to encourage candidates, video responses are considered permissible in the recruiting process. It is important to note that organizations who expect candidates to create videos should also give candidates an opportunity to continue through the recruiting process *without* creating a video. In addition, any hiring decisions should be based on documented data including videos so if the need

---

60. Carol R. Miaskoff, "EEOC Informal Discussion Letter," U.S. Equal Employment Opportunity Commission, last modified November 4, 2010.

arises that requires an audit of the decision, an authorized third party can review candidate information and videos to determine if any form of bias occurred. When an organization hires for grit, it is critically important that the focus be on reducing bias and creating opportunity for all.

It is important during the hiring process that you are able to justify and explain decisions made and that those decisions have been made impartially and without biases. There are a lot of variables and stakeholders involved in the hiring process and, as such, organizations should be able to demonstrate why one candidate was hired over the other. When there are many variables that need to be taken into account, there is bound to be human bias that is introduced even through error. If an organization uses an automated and consistent approach to engage all candidates, it can greatly reduce bias especially in the early stages of the process.

In addition, an organization has to be able to demonstrate why an applicant was *not* considered for the position. If an organization just looks at resumes to select candidates that proceed to the next step of the process, that can be subjective and harder to support if any questions arise. If an organization uses job simulations and gives every candidate a chance, the same chance, the decision can be supported by data and responses of the candidate. Also, comparing candidates and basing any decisions from that comparison can be done by looking at the actual job simulation tasks. The responses give hiring managers and recruiters a better chance of reducing bias.

One of the most effective ways *Hire for Grit* reduces bias and increases diversity is by following an automated engagement process consistently as soon as a candidate applies. What one recruiter may consider characteristics of an outstanding candidate, another might not. What one organization believes to be ideal experiences, another might not. By adopting the *Hire for Grit* approach, you are ensuring a consistent hiring method. The job simulation-based approach is a critical part of that consistency. When I spoke with Jay Laabs, CEO of Spaulding Ridge, his message was unequivocal:

> "The higher education model has changed dramatically and giving everyone a chance to demonstrate their fit for the role based on broader life experiences is more sustainable over time."

Evaluating candidates is far easier if consistency across the hiring process is automatically applied.

Benefit: Save Time and Money

So far, we have looked at how hiring for grit helps organizations reduce bias, increase diversity and inclusion. What about the cost of hiring and the time to fill? Many organizations look at it to measure the effectiveness of their recruiting efforts.

According to detailed research done by the Glassdoor Economic Research Group in 2017 the average time to fill for a role by any given industry for most countries ranges in the four to six week timeframe.[61]

---

61. Dr. Andrew Chamberlain, "How Long Does It Take to Hire? Interview Duration in 25 Countries," *Economic Research* (blog), *Glassdoor*, August 9, 2017.

As per the Society for Human Resources Management's (SHRM) Human Capital Benchmarking Report, the average time to fill a given position is forty-two days and the average cost-per-hire is $4,129.[62] The cost-per-hire can actually be much greater for hard to fill positions and when you take into account the cost of not hiring on time, the number can skyrocket.

It is critical for organizations to reduce the time it takes to hire candidates without compromising on the quality of hires. To increase recruiting efficiency, some questions that organizations may consider are:

- How long does it take to hire for a position? Does the number vary greatly by position or role?
- How does that time break down? If it takes forty-two days to fill a role, where is the forty-two days spent? What part of the forty-two days is spent waiting for candidates versus waiting internally to collaborate and make decisions?
- How much of the time spent can be automated to increase efficiency?
- What types of tasks are performed internally during the time to fill?
- What is the cost of hire for your organization? Did you take into account the time and resources it takes from start to finish?
- What is the cost of not making a decision on time? How much does it cost your organization each day that the position remains unfilled?

---

62. Society of Human Resource Managment, "Average Cost-per-Hire for Companies Is $4,129, Shrm Survey Finds," SHRM press release, August 3, 2016.

Three Core Drivers of Hiring For Grit

1. Automating the *boring parts* of the recruiting process

Some of the boring parts of the recruiting process can include asking questions around logistics and must have requirements. What shifts are you available to work? Do you have a driver's license? When are you available to start? It may also include the coordination tasks of getting candidates scheduled for interviews, sending them reminders, collaborating with internal team members, candidate feedback, and so many other tasks that require access to information in an organized manner. Collecting such information in an easy and automated way can help reduce the time to fill for a position.

Automating boring tasks can help organizations consider the time and effort put into career fairs. The typical career fair involves a bit of prep work, which could be automated to a certain degree; however, the real value is in rethinking the experience during the career fair.

Imagine this experience during a career fair:

- *Loud and noisy environment where candidates wait in line to speak with a recruiter.*
- *The recruiter has to take a quick glance at their resume and ask them some quick questions.*
- *The recruiter has to make a call quickly about the candidate fit and add the resume to a "call back" or "not the right fit" pile.*
- *The entire communication happens in seconds or minutes in an environment that is not conducive to a meaningful conversation.*

- *The engagement across all candidates may not be consistent especially as the day goes on.*
- *Once the day is over, recruiters are exhausted and often have to sift through the resumes and do manual data entry of their notes/next steps in the process.*

Now, contrast that experience with one that leverages automation and creates an engagement process consistent to all candidates:

- *Before a candidate even shows up at the career fair, they are shown videos that showcase the organization, the positions that are open, and they are asked to RSVP and upload their resume.*
- *When the candidate visits the organization's booth at the career fair, there is a self check-in process/sign. If they haven't previously RSVP'd, they can text to apply, watch the videos, and pick the right position that they are interested in.*
- *The self check-in process/sign reduces or completely eliminates wait times.*
- *Every candidate that expresses interest for a position is shown videos and asked a series of job simulation questions.*
- *Any resumes uploaded by the candidates get automatically indexed and made fully searchable. No more piles of "call back" or "not the right fit" resumes.*
- *The candidates can respond to the questions directly from their smartphones and document their question in a systematic way.*
- *Once the candidates are done answering the questions, the recruiter can review them quickly from their smartphone, ask any follow-up questions and discuss next steps with the candidates.*

- *Any further review of the candidate profile by hiring managers and other stakeholders can be performed systematically without the need for recruiters to debrief them by emailing and sending them the candidate resumes and notes.*

The above example is just a simple process in which automation can be used to make everyone's experience and life easier. Automation is not intended to *replace* the human connection, but instead *enhance* the human connection. We have all seen the efficiencies that automation can bring to our lives when we think about applications like Google Maps or the check-in experience at the airline counters at the airport. Automation is something we should constantly be thinking about to create efficient processes and produce better experiences. Recruiting automation is a very important strategic initiative that every organization should consider.

2. Creating and collaborating on a 360-degree view of the candidate application

You may have experienced the back and forth that recruiters, hiring managers, and other stakeholders experience when evaluating a candidate. The process can require a fair bit of coordination and is often reliant on just a resume and some verbal feedback that is shared about a candidate.

We have already discussed how resumes aren't the most effective way to tell a candidate's story and determine the fit for the role. Having a system and process to review a candidate's feedback about the job simulations presented to them gives hiring managers and recruiters more information to make an informed decision. Instead of just reviewing the resumes and interview notes, a hiring manager can collaborate better with more data points and decide which candidates to focus on.

In addition, leveraging unbiased simple filters that can help zero-in on the candidates can be a huge time saver. If the number of candidates received for a position is more than twenty, the time savings can be even bigger. With a few clicks, a hiring manager can filter candidates that spent five minutes working on the simulations, answer questions that are important for a successful transition to the new role and zoom in on new candidates that have gone through the process since the hiring manager's last review. Once complete, a hiring manager can then collaborate directly in the system with the recruiters and other stakeholders to provide their feedback. When interviewing the candidate, the recruiter and hiring manager follow the interview guidelines and document the feedback for others to review so subsequent meetings with the candidate can be informational. If there are any additional questions that need to be asked, they can be based on the feedback already received.

Having a 360-degree view of a candidate's performance can lead to a tremendous amount of time savings.

3. Reducing candidate wait times

The number one complaint that all candidates have is once they apply for a job, they never hear back. This creates a terrible experience for the candidate and can tarnish an employer's brand amongst applicants and future hires.

Any organization that recruits talent should make it a priority to be responsive to candidates and reduce any wait times. It becomes harder to respond as more candidates apply for the role. Hence leveraging automation, personalized engagement, and texting platforms that candidates prefer to use, all of which can make a big difference in reducing any candidate wait times. In a labor market where organizations are competing over talent, being responsive and personalized can make all the difference.

We can learn many lessons about reducing wait times for candidates by looking at what companies are doing to reduce wait times for their customers. Any company that has a call center tracks metrics like call duration, call wait times, call resolutions metrics, customer satisfaction post call, and others. Such metrics can help a company stay ahead of their competition and ensure customers stay happy.

The same type of a mindset needs to be adopted by organizations that recruit talent. In a job market where talent reigns supreme, candidates are more like customers than ever before and organizations should respond and engage with candidates just like they would with customers. Companies leverage automation platforms like customer relationship management systems, marketing automation systems, and customer service systems to create a better experience for customers. Organizations should leverage recruiting automation and engagement platforms in a similar fashion and track the effectiveness of the engagement.

When you hire for grit, the number of candidates dramatically increases due to the widening of the recruiting funnel and since every candidate is given a proper chance for the position, it creates a more robust candidate experience that results in the reduction of candidate wait times. When you hire for grit, it is less about the candidate waiting to hear from the company and more about the candidate responding to the requests by the company. Such a reversal in the wait also helps companies measure the pro-activeness of the candidates. In this chapter we reviewed the benefits that result in hiring for grit. By leveraging the strategies of hiring for grit, organizations can reduce bias, increase diversity and widen their recruiting funnel in this tight labor market. In addition, organizations can reduce the time and cost of hiring talent even though the volume of candidates may dramatically increase. *Hire for Grit* creates a better experience for all parties involved and it allows recruiting stakeholders to make informed decisions.

CHAPTER 10

THINKING OUTSIDE THE RECRUITING BOX

———

Have you wondered what you can do to widen your recruiting funnel or not rely on the same recruiting channels that everyone else does?

How can you reach candidates that are in most need of opportunity and could make great additions to your team, however they simply don't have access to the resources to even know about your job openings?

How can you source diverse talent more effectively?

These are some of the questions that I have often pondered. My work with companies like Six Flags, Tapecon, Capital Management Services, Doyle Security, BryLin Hospital, and others have inspired some innovative strategies to come up with real answers to create more opportunities for all and truly widening the top end of your recruiting funnel.

But widening the top of a recruiting funnel also means that organizations have to be prepared for the increase in candidates. To do so, organizations can leverage the power of hiring for grit by creating a standardized process less reliant on humans having to make an **initial** call on who gets a chance and more reliant on the candidates demonstrating their interest and abilities for the role.

If your organization wants to increase diversity in your recruiting efforts within the community, what can you do? Here are some ideas you may want to consider:

- If you are looking to hire from certain community neighborhoods, consider purchasing ads at bus stops and on buses that drive through those communities. Imagine seeing an ad which says, "We are hiring, text GRIT to 716-247-4629!" which initiates the *Hire for Grit* process.
- Imagine partnering with community organizations that enable training and apprenticeships. Imagine creating business cards that can be handed out to constituents that say, "We are hiring hard working people who want to learn and grow. Text GRIT to 716-247-4629!"
- There is a serious shortage of diverse talent in the tech community. Consider purchasing billboards that have an analytical problem that potential candidates could solve. What if billboard signs said, "We are hiring! Text the largest prime number you know to 716-247-4629 to see if you could excel in a technology career."
- Organizations can also leverage the power of social media to create targeted ads by geography, under-represented members of a team, etc., to encourage them to text or message to apply and go through the process. Imagine seeing an Instagram or TikTok which said something

such as "Here is a problem. Solve it and we will interview you ASAP! Text us…"

There are many strategies organizations can implement to widen their recruiting funnel. Recruiting doesn't just mean posting an ad on Indeed, LinkedIn, and other syndication platforms. There are creative ways to reaching a wider and often under-represented candidate audience.

Another important consideration when hiring for grit is exploring parallels that exist between roles that you may be hiring for and other unrelated jobs. If you are hiring for a financial advisor, who must have interpersonal relationship building skills, would you consider a barista for the role? If a barista is someone that is trained and spends their day building positive and meaningful experiences for customers, could that person become a great financial advisor if you could teach them the basics of finance? Here is another example. Could bank tellers make great software quality assurance (QA) engineers? Bank tellers have to clearly be methodical, organized, and analytical enough to find the root cause of any reconciliation errors. If you take away any software skills (which can be taught with access to the right resources) could that mean that companies could tap into a talent pool previously unconsidered for QA engineers?

The key message here is that when hiring for grit, organizations should rely less on experience in job titles that match the role they are hiring for and identify transferable skills that could be a great way to widen the funnel. Most importantly, widening the funnel gives you the opportunity to rely on *Hire for Grit* framework to minimize your workload and reduce any assumptions you make when hiring. This approach makes it less about "I think this candidate would be a good fit because they have worked as a _____ in the past" and more about "This candidate has clearly demonstrated they have the right skills or ability to learn for this role. Let's interview them."

Tapecon is a manufacturing company in Buffalo, NY that has embraced the *Hire for Grit* approach when recruiting. When I spoke to Steve Davis about his vision and company's approach to hiring, the following themes permeate all parts of their organizations:

- "When hiring, think outside the candidate pool."
- "You can't see passion on a piece of paper/resume."
- "A candidate's fit for the role is a two-way street where both the company and the candidate should proactively decide whether it makes sense." It is about "Hiring each other."

Steve Davis and his team at Tapecon have an inspiring story to share with all manufacturers who are struggling to find talent. Talent is out there. Perhaps the challenges organizations face for not being able to hire fast enough are derived from factors such as recruiting funnels being too narrow. Maybe even because we aren't being creative enough in how we assess someone's fit for the role or because organizations don't inspire people to consider applying if they don't view themselves as the "right fit" on paper.

Using videos is another way for organizations to hire for grit. We have already discussed any bias related concerns about using videos. The focus of the video should be to clearly demonstrate a candidate's fit based on a company's culture and values. Even though it hasn't been verified by Southwest Airlines, over the years there have been several documented instances of pilots being asked to wear their favorite "brown shorts" as part of the recruiting process to see if the candidate pilots would fit into the "fun culture" of Southwest. Shorts are part of the Southwest summer uniform and considered too relaxed by some of the pilots who often regard their suit and tie uniform as an important part of their job. Organizations should consider what represents their "brown shorts" and allow candidates to demonstrate their fit based on the culture and values. It is important to note that organizations should not use videos as the only determining factor, but rather as an opportunity for candidates to tell their story using another channel.

Job fairs are another part of the recruiting process that you can consider adjusting as part of your *Hire for Grit* initiative. A common sight during the job fair is the line of people waiting to speak with a company representative(s). The representatives end up speaking with hundreds of candidates only to go back to the office with a blur, not remembering anything about the whirlwind day. In addition to the poor experience for candidates and recruiters, the interaction is often a few minutes long which includes having to consciously or unconsciously decide what pile to put the candidate's resume in: "call back" or "reject." There is simply no way to know if a candidate is the right fit for the role during a quick interaction in a noisy environment with unlimited distractions.

Is there a better way to manage the job fair process by applying the *Hire for Grit* framework?

Yes! Organizations can start with showing all the candidates that are interested in speaking with representatives a set of videos which outlines some of the common questions that are expected. This can happen in a virtual environment *prior* to the career fair. If a candidate is interested, he or she can simply text and go through the series of videos and questions that the organization can use as a pre-interview. The candidates that complete the questions and watch the videos talking about the opportunities can then be invited for a longer in-person interview during the career fair. This way, the company representatives are focused on the strong candidates and can give them enough time and attention while in person. During those conversations, the commentary should focus less on generic questions and rather on the specific answers that the candidate has already provided.

It's a bit like the Khan Academy model. You go to class and ask questions when you have made a sincere attempt at self-learning. But that's how active learning happens! The *Hire for Grit* model is based on a similar idea: give everyone a chance, ask them to work on what matters before you meet them, and then focus on the candidates based on real performance and growth mindset challenges.

Using the strategies described above, organizations can make the job fair's experience much better for all parties, saving time and quickly zeroing-in on the right candidates.

One of the final considerations about hiring for grit is masking candidate information before a human reviews their answers. Imagine seeing answers to questions and other relevant information on how the candidate took on the challenges encountered in the questions without first seeing a candidate's name and other identifiable information. This way, all candidates get the same fair chance, and the chance of any biases being introduced when a recruiter and hiring manager review their answers is also greatly reduced. Any unmasking of the candidate's identifiable data should be clearly documented. Audits can easily be put in place which ensure that candidate dispositions were made *before* the candidate's identifiable information was unmasked. According to an article published in the American Economic Review, when doing "blind auditions" the number of female musicians in the five highest ranked orchestras in the US increased 6 percent.[63] We have talked a lot about giving everyone a fair chance and then deciding on the next steps for a candidate based on their responses. What strategies can an organization use to determine who the strong candidates are? Some strategies that GRITSEED customers have deployed are:

- Look at the amount of quality time a candidate puts into the process of answering the questions. Did they just rush through it or were the answers methodical and effort driven?
- How did they answer questions that they may not have been qualified to answer? Did they just say "I don't know" or did they say "I don't know, but here is the research I did to learn and based on that I believe the answer to be..."
- When hiring salespeople, if you asked them to redo a problem because you expected better of them, do they handle rejection well and try again? Do they spend less or more time the second time around?
- How do they respond to questions? Does their response come across as someone who could hold a conversation well with your customers and other team members?
- How did the candidate demonstrate what they know about the hiring organization? Did the candidate make

---

63. Claudia Goldin and Cecelia Rouse, "Orchestrating Impartiality: The Impact of 'Blind' Auditions on Female Musicians," *American Economic Review* 90, no. 4 (September 2000): 715-741.

it a generic pitch or was it aligned with the organization's core business and values?

In this chapter, we have explored several considerations with respect to hiring for grit. We've discussed strategies to widen recruiting funnels, sourcing across different channels and giving candidates a chance based off simulations and not what they look like on paper. We have also reviewed how videos and updated job fair processes can help streamline recruiting and attract the right talent. Finally, we reviewed how masking identifiable candidate information in the recruiting process can lead to a more diverse workforce.

CHAPTER 11

HIRING TECHNICAL TALENT USING GRIT

If you have tried hiring for a technical role, you know how hard it is. In the US and in many parts of the world, there simply aren't enough people who are technically trained compared to the number of open technology jobs.

If there aren't enough technically trained people, is it possible to hire non-technical people for technical roles and make sure they are effective? Is it possible to hire people that trained in non-technical areas and hire them for technical roles?

Over the last ten years, I have personally hired people with non-technical backgrounds who have become excellent software developers, quality assurance engineers, technical consultants and more. You may remember the story of Pete from the Introduction or the story of Jason in Chapter Two where I introduced the meaning of grit. There are many other examples of people that I have hired who wouldn't have been hired, if we had not followed the *Hire for Grit* framework.

Some other hiring stories are of people like:

- A roofer who became a cloud computing software developer
- An Olive Garden server who became a quality assurance engineer
- A bank analyst that transformed into a highly skilled Salesforce.com consultant
- A manufacturing line worker who became a cloud computing software developer
- A math major with no programming background who wrote high quality code
- A college grad with a 2.0 GPA repeatedly turned down for opportunities but became a highly respected member of the technical staff
- A philosophy major who went on to lead a large technical team
- A graduate with an associate degree transitioned into one of the most productive programmers
- A refugee who barely spoke English that became a Salesforce.com certified professional
- A grocery store worker with an MBA who became a quality assurance analyst
- A channel sales person who became a highly sought after Salesforce.com consultant

The list goes on. I want to emphasize that each of the examples above are from real people that I have hired whose lives were changed because I hired them for their grit.

I wanted to share specific details of how I used the *Hire for Grit* framework to hire technical people. My hope in sharing these examples is that it will inspire you to hire people for technical roles who may not look like the right fit when you evaluate their background and resume, but who can become some of your best technical hires with the proper training.

Non-Technical Talent with Grit

When hiring for technical roles, I base my hiring decisions on four core beliefs. Let's review each one in detail and walk-through real examples of how I hired for grit this way.

1. Becoming a good technical professional is highly dependent on being patient, committed, analytical, and curious

Every technical professional knows that one must have patience when working through technical problems. Often times, things don't go right the first time. You have to debug code, rewrite code, analyze what went wrong; and for all those types of tasks, you have to be patient and committed. When I hired for Cloud62, Huron Consulting and GRITSEED, I created job simulations that required a deep level of patience and commitment from candidates. I would ask questions that didn't have a straightforward answer. I would then analyze how they answered the questions. Did they give up quickly and say "I don't know" or did they keep trying when they ran into a dead end? How long did they work on a problem?

I found that people with a liberal arts background (e.g., linguistics, philosophy) were excellent at being logical, analytical, and curious thinkers. When I couldn't give them a programming problem, I would often give them a Sudoku problem to solve (with rules if they needed them) or even asked them brainteaser types of questions. When they solved the brainteaser problem, I would analyze *how* they worked through the problem and not whether they got it right or wrong.

In some cases, before making a final decision to hire, I would often give job simulations relating to real technical problems and asked them what kinds of resources they could use to help solve them. What I wanted to learn was how curious a candidate was and how resourceful they were in seeking out solutions. Did they try simple Google searches? Did they look at common technical boards, like Stack Overflow? Were they able to review a reference documentation and know what part to focus on?

A large part of being a technical professional is being curious and constantly learning. One needs to continue seeking out solutions to problems that you encounter every day at work. One must have the right grit factor to be able to persevere through the problems in a systematic way and keep learning.

2. Most problems can eventually be solved using a playbook and simple rules.

Some of the most successful technical professionals I have worked with have been experts at following playbooks and simple rules when solving problems. Following a playbook involves creating a plan before jumping in headfirst. Executing the playbook means sticking to the plan and having the ability to know when the plan needs to be tweaked.

When hiring, I created job simulations about situations that often arose at work. The job simulations covered topics like "How would you handle an outage at work?" I would then analyze how candidates responded. Did they focus on getting the right team resources to help? Did they think about the customer and keeping them informed? Did they think about a backup plan in case their plan didn't work?

A common rule that I have seen most technical professionals follow is breaking a big problem into smaller ones. When evaluating a candidate's fit for the role, I considered how they tried solving a large problem. Breaking it down into smaller ones, finding patterns, and trying to extrapolate data are common practices that successful candidates followed. What I also learned was that candidates that have solved real life problems, like remodeling a house, were very good at breaking down big problems into smaller ones and following a playbook.

In addition to breaking big problems into smaller ones and solving the smaller ones, the most successful candidates would find patterns and use those patterns in solving the problems. A common job simulation I would give to candidates is "If you know X has happened in the past, how would you go about solving Y?" I would then analyze their ability to see the pattern between X and Y. People that found the patterns were often faster at solving technical problems compared to highly trained technical members of the team. People that solved problems through pattern matching were also great at learning from past mistakes and ensuring that code they wrote in the future would take past learnings into account. Such an approach resulted in some of the most resilient code I have seen written.

I have also seen some of the most successful technical professionals follow the assumption that the key is understanding the assumptions that they are making when solving a problem and identifying when those assumptions fall apart. A common job simulation I used for this type of assessment was evaluating if the candidate understood how a customer would use a product or service that they developed. Did they assume that the customer would use it in a way that was based on sound footing? Would they consider a customer using a product in a way that was outside of the norm? How would they handle such situations?

Some of the best non-technical people I hired relied on their life experiences to work on the job simulations I gave them. They applied rules, like breaking a large problem into smaller ones and they also had the ability to understand the assumptions they were making in trying to solve the problem. In many ways, the most successful candidates had "learned how to learn and solve problems" through life experiences and/or their non-technical educational journey.

3. Having a successful technical career doesn't require a computer science or engineering degree

I graduated with an undergraduate degree in computer science over twenty years ago. So much has changed since then. Dozens of highly sophisticated programming languages have been invented. Easy to use frameworks have been created and access to online documentation and resources have increased exponentially. Most recently, cloud platforms like Amazon Web Services (AWS), Microsoft Azure, and Google Cloud have created Lego block-like components which require minimal computer science skills and the ability to put pre-existing Lego blocks together and apply minimal customization.

The change in skills needed to be successful in technical careers has also changed dramatically. It is less about inventing algorithms and more about reusing components that have made life easier for any technical professional to build sophisticated software. Don't get me wrong, there is a great need for computer scientists; however, there are lots of jobs where you don't need to invent and analyze algorithms to get the job done.

When hiring technical talent, I have created job simulations that rely on existing platform offerings from AWS. When hiring someone for a machine learning role, which is considered highly advanced, I have considered math majors. I have given them pointers to freely available AWS machine learning libraries to see if they can use them in a black box capacity. Ultimately the goal of the job simulation is to get candidates to solve a simple machine learning problem to classify an object in a video or picture. The key point is that in the technical world we live in today, resources are limitless and access to those resources are now free for the user or almost free. What matters is a candidate's ability to take minimal direction and move in the right direction.

I have also found that candidates that have done well in job simulations are typically really good at keeping up with the change that is ever present in most technical disciplines. Staying adaptable is almost mission critical. After hiring Pete, he has gone on to learn all the latest capabilities of Salesforce. com's analytics platforms on his own, simply by tinkering and attempting. That ability to learn and accept change has led him to have a highly successful YouTube channel.

As you consider hiring non-technical talent for your technical roles, give them access to resources, some direction, and see what comes out of it. I am sure there will be people that don't enjoy the exercise. As we have discussed, that's part of the *Hire for Grit* process, but through that same process, you will find people that make sense of the technical Lego blocks, dig into the resources given to them, and make magic happen.

4. Being able to communicate your ideas to others and listening to feedback can make a huge difference in one's career

Perhaps the most important capability I have looked for when hiring anyone has been their ability to communicate and listen effectively. Additionally, being able to express one's ideas and thoughts in a concise and cohesive way is mission critical for technical roles. When designing products, systems, and services, you have to digest incredible amounts of information and then express your thoughts to members of the team, customers, and other stakeholders.

If I hire for technical roles, I have often used job simulations that purposely provided too much information and then analyzed how a candidate focused on the right pieces of data. In addition, I have asked candidates to write in their own words what they learned after reviewing all that data. What I found is liberal arts majors were excellent at reviewing vast amounts of data and having the ability to slice it and dice it with different points of view.

Another common job simulation I utilized was in-person or virtual whiteboarding sessions. I would describe in person or record a video describing a problem on a whiteboard, then hand over the whiteboard marker to the candidate. If the simulation was in person, I would then observe that candidate to see if he or she got up and went to the whiteboard or if they stayed seated. Did they attempt to understand the problem further and ask questions? Did they think out loud? Did they try different solutions? How did they explain what they were trying to do? When I gave them feedback, did they listen and adjust their thinking or did they simply push back? The dynamics of the back and forth when solving a real problem in person or even virtually (synchronously or asynchronously) gave us a very a good understanding of what it would be like to work with that person.

We found that people with a background in team sports were excellent communicators. Sports taught those candidates empathy and the ability to truly connect with others at a deeper level. We often sought out candidates who had played a team sport in high school or college. In addition to sports, we saw that candidates who had worked while in high school or college were also excellent communicators. If they had experienced working with customers and other team members during their early work years, their ability to handle job simulations dramatically improved.

Some of the best non-technical people I have hired had a unique ability to digest vast amounts of information and then ask very targeted meaningful questions. A big difference between people we hired and the ones we didn't was what they asked when we gave them job simulations. Did they ask general questions or were they very specific showing they had done the prerequisite work. When someone asks questions, you get a good idea about their mindset and the work they have already done before they got to the question. It's not just about the initial set of questions, but the back and forth that transpires when you answer their questions. Candidates who were naturally curious and excellent communicators have turned out to be some of the best technical members of my team.

Training and Support

So far, we have reviewed some of the approaches we took in hiring non-technical people for technical roles. In addition to selecting the right candidates, it was also important to provide the candidates with the right training and support so they could become effective members of the team. The people that we ended up hiring were self-starters and excellent learners who hit the ground running with minimal direction. Our job was to help them set a foundation by focusing on learning the technical skills that mattered and prescribing a plan to learn those skills.

We didn't have to reinvent the wheel around training. Websites like Udemy and others provide a step-by-step approach to learning almost any technical skill. Udemy provides courses with step-by-step instructions and hands-on exercises for AWS engineers, Python developers, Quality Assurance analysts and others. Companies like Salesforce. com even offer totally free Trailblazer online courses to learn about the Salesforce.com platform. We used these same tools when training new recruits at Cloud62 and Huron Consulting.

We provided our recruits with access to online courses and then did daily check-ins with them to answer their questions. On a weekly basis, we would do demo jams where the candidates would showcase what they had learned that week. A demo session would involve describing what the recruit worked out, showcasing code, running code, and describing the lessons learned through mistakes they made. Having the demo sessions helped the recruits learn, communicate, and gather feedback from senior members of the team. We used tools like Atlassian's Confluence wiki software to document each candidate's progress, findings, and collective learnings so the next group of recruits hired could build on the learnings of the last.

We learned through this process that if we stuck to hiring for grit and used the appropriate job simulations in making informed hiring decisions, the quality of the hires was incredible. They were able to learn and be productive members of the team often in as little as three months. Once we felt comfortable that a recruit was ready, we would start by giving them real product development or quality assurance tasks and assigned them to a mentor who would be able to assist them through the process. We learned that the best learning experience for the recruits resulted from writing and committing code and seeing the features that were developed in use by real customers. It was an incredible feeling for the recruits and for the team at large.

As we wrap up this chapter, I want to challenge you to think differently when hiring technical talent. We have such a massive need for technical talent today and there are people everywhere who have the potential to become technical ninjas looking for opportunity. Why not consider non-technical people for technical roles? Why not give everyone a chance to showcase what they can do? Why not hire people and create opportunity while reducing the technical talent shortage? Change can start with you. If you are a hiring manager looking for technical resources, hiring for grit is a good starting point to find that diamond you are looking for.

CHAPTER 12

HIRE FOR GRIT FAQS

———

Over the last several years, I have spoken with hundreds of organizations about hiring for grit. We have learned and partnered together in tremendous ways discussing some common questions. I wanted to outline them here so as you read the book or once you are done, you can reference them at will. Think of these questions as the starting point of hiring for grit. There are no right or wrong answers, but the answers are based on the core beliefs. As a summary, the core beliefs that we have reviewed previously in the book are:

1. *Everyone that expresses interest in a position should be given a fair chance to demonstrate that they can perform the role and responsibilities. What the candidate does with the chance is up to them.*

2. *We now live in a world where we have access to constant streams of information, making it easier for people to learn almost any new skill through platforms such as YouTube, Udemy, Coursera, and many other Massive Open Online Courses [MOOC]. Therefore, hiring should not be about the information a candidate holds, but*

*what they choose to do with that information. Some-
one with grit and a growth mindset can learn new skills
quicker and more effectively.*

3. *There are thousands of "underemployed" talented people
all over the world, many of whom have the potential and
capability to do much more than what they are pursuing
today. It is important to look beyond previous job titles
and instead focus on character and attitude or an organization will continue to hire from the same pool of people.*

4. *Hiring for character and mindset is far more important in the long term than hiring for skill. Skills can be
learned and taught. Whereas, hard work ethic, grit,
growth mindset, and other character pillars are acquired
through years of life experiences. This should be the focal
point of the hiring process.*

How do you measure grit?

There is no magic formula to measure grit. There is no test
or personality assessment to measure one's grit. There is no
comparison of grit from one person to the other. In fact, it is
important for organizations to realize that the "standardized
test" approach to grading or evaluating someone can actually
be flawed and biased itself. I have never believed in the model
of ranking and judging people based on a set of hypotheticals
or evaluation criteria that doesn't apply to everyone.

There is a simpler approach that leads to better and more
informed decisions about hiring. When organizations inform
candidates about job-related tasks and simulations, candidates learn more about the position than a job description
ever can. After sharing information with all candidates in

a consistent way, organizations can then ask the candidates relevant questions that reveal whether or not they would be a good fit for the role.

If a candidate is truly interested in the position and the role, they will go through the series of job-related questions and tasks that an organization poses them. That is where the grit comes in. Does the candidate have the grit to complete what is asked of them? Will the candidate attempt to answer questions that at first may be challenging for them, but require a growth mindset? Will the candidate give up, or will the candidate have the awareness to realize that the role may not be a right fit for them after learning more about the position?

I have learned, through my interactions with thousands of candidates, that individuals who have grit are the ones who demonstrate a growth mindset, take on the questions that are presented as learning opportunities and demonstrate their value much better than a resume ever could.

Grit is less about a quantifiable number and a destination and more about the journey they experience and its ups and downs.

Will candidates perform the tasks and job simulations?

I get this question a lot. In this tight labor market, where candidates have dozens of career options, will they perform job-related tasks and simulations?

At GRITSEED, we have had over one hundred thousand candidates go through the *Hire for Grit* process. Many of them completed all the tasks that were assigned to them. Many saw the simulations as a great opportunity to engage with organizations to learn more about the position. The candidates that performed the tasks, invested the time and energy, had a much higher chance of getting hired.

Using job tasks and simulations are also an effective strategy to reduce mis-hires. Mis-hires cost organizations millions a year and the flip side to it for candidates is also equally disruptive. Mis-hiring and attrition results in loss of confidence and tremendous stress for new hires! Isn't it better to make an informed decision about the position where the candidate has had a chance to decide if they are really interested and if an organization has had a chance to see how a candidate would perform if they were hired? It is in everyone's best interest to prevent mis-hires.

I have come across many candidates who wanted to become software developers but didn't really have a background in programming. When they went through the *Hire for Grit* process, they got frustrated with the programming and troubleshooting to solve the problems and realized that software development wasn't for them. That is totally okay. Those candidates went on to pursue careers that interested them and made them happier.

That said, I also understand that if an organization is looking for talent that is highly specialized, and not readily available with tons of career options, they may choose to completely opt out of this type of a process. That is understandable. When hiring for grit, an organization should have an idea about the number of candidates they will get for a specific position. Based on that number, organizations should create a process that is rightfully suited. If the recruiting funnel is very wide at the top and narrow on the bottom, then a longer, multi-step process is suited to truly find the candidates who are interested in the position. If the recruiting funnel is narrow at the top and very wide at the bottom, then use the *Hire for Grit* approach to better engage with the limited talent by creating a better and more easier experience for them. Make an impression on those candidates so your organization can stand out compared to all the others that may have just posted a job description about the position. Wouldn't it be awesome for highly competitive candidates to see messages via video about the position from the highest levels of the organization? Wouldn't that create a better experience?

Hiring for grit works in this tight labor market. Hiring for grit can also work well if there is an abundance of talent.

Can you prove that the Hire for Grit approach is not biased?

First, before I attempt to even answer this question, let's be clear: one of the core objectives of the *Hire for Grit* approach is to help organizations reduce bias, improve on inclusion and help increase candidate and hire diversity. The "why" behind *Hire for Grit* and GRITSEED is that reason.

That said, no system or process can completely remove conscious or unconscious biases that exist around us. What we can do is bring transparency, consistency, and decision criteria that is based on evaluation techniques that build on transparency and consistency for the applicant cohort. If every candidate that applies using the *Hire for Grit* approach is given a chance regardless of their background, then bias is not introduced at that step of the process because of the consistency chance given to all. If an organization doesn't use the *Hire for Grit* approach, then there is a strong chance of bias being introduced in the process early on when a recruiter has to make the call to get back to the candidate or after not having reviewed their resume. Hiring for grit helps reduce that bias early in the recruiting cycle.

Hiring for grit is about making informed hiring decisions. It is not about using AI to make the decision for you or to plot a candidate on some chart which compares them to others using some kind of a percentile approach. That is totally unnecessary since candidates remove themselves from the process by not completing it. Since the focus is on candidates who are a true fit for the role, the ones that actually do demonstrate their capabilities should be reviewed by the recruiter and hiring manager. The questions, tasks, and job simulations should pertain to the job functions and ones that would be performed by all that are hired. Focusing on the actual "to-dos" vs. some hypothetical extrapolation of years of experience or credentials in determining one's ability to perform the job leads to less bias.

What if the candidates don't have access to a computer? When organizations use the *Hire for Grit* approach, they must provide candidates the ability to request alternative approaches to completing the process. A good example of that is providing access to technology and resources that may be specific to a role and not readily available.

To further reduce bias, organizations can choose to hide identifiable information that can lead to bias. Hiding names until truly necessary is a great way to ensure that the people involved in the hiring process are basing their judgement on who to move forward based on non-identifiable data.

By introducing transparency and consistency to the process, if the need does arise to audit why hiring decisions were made over others, organizations using the *Hire for Grit* approach are able to provide the necessary objective criteria and evidence needed to prove or disprove a claim.

Finally, as mentioned earlier, no system can ever be 100 percent free from bias and the objective should be focused on reducing the bias through a non-judgmental, consistent and transparent approach to giving all candidates a chance.

Doesn't the use of videos actually increase bias based on identifiable information like age, race, gender?

If organizations strictly use videos to make hiring decisions, then yes, that could lead to bias. I have strongly advocated the use of videos in the *Hire for Grit* approach to create a more inclusive representation of the work, job duties, and culture. By not just relying on job descriptions and publicly available information about the company, videos are a great way for a company to inform candidates about the role.

If videos are used consistently with all candidates, then they can create a level playing field for all candidates to tell their story. Organizations must also provide the candidates the opportunity to opt out if they choose not to use videos. They must not use this as a form of bias when making a decision about the applicant.

Finally, using videos can be thought of as an in-person interview. The same bias that can happen during in-person interviews could also happen in videos, but because the *Hire for Grit* approach means that everyone is given a chance to demonstrate their capabilities, everything gets documented and is tracked systematically. If bias does happen and needs to be investigated, you can go back through the process and address the concerns.

How does hiring for grit widen the recruiting funnel?

You widen the recruiting funnel in several ways:

First, when you hire for grit, you remove the unnecessary dependance on dis-qualifiers in job descriptions that would limit people who apply. Organizations often use years of experience as a way to weed out candidates and un-consciously discourage candidates from applying. If that didn't happen, more candidates would apply than an organization could review and handle. With the *Hire for Grit* approach, the goal is to draft job descriptions to get as many people as possible to apply. Since a systematic way of engaging with candidates has to be put in place as part of the process, there is no added burden on existing staff to review all the candidates. Recruiting automation and engagement platforms like GRITSEED take care of that.

Secondly, everyone automatically gets a chance when hiring for grit. Giving candidates the opportunity to demonstrate their fit for your role increases your total candidate count.

Organizations can actually target candidate cohorts, neighborhoods or even existing under-employed talent that may have transferable skills encouraging them to go through the process. At GRITSEED, we have seen organizations advertise for roles in low-income neighborhoods to help drive more opportunity. This allowed the organizations to consider candidates that would have not normally applied. A great example of this type of advertising is to use bus stop billboards or bus banners to get candidates to apply via text.

Finally, the *Hire for Grit* approach core belief "access to information is no longer the problem and what candidates do with the information should be the focus" means that candidates who may not be the exact fit for the position can still be given a chance to learn and become adept at the skills necessary to excel at the job.

Is hiring for grit just for technical roles?

Hiring for grit is for many types of jobs. Some of the common roles that organizations have filled using the *Hire for Grit* approach are software developers, machinists, customer service agents, hospitality workers, registered nurses, healthcare providers, financial advisors, insurance sales representatives, and many more.

Hire for Grit is not intended for jobs which require advanced credentials like physicians or lawyers *but* you can still use this type of approach to quickly assess if the credentialed talents fit the role and to quickly engage with them. In a tight labor market where nurses are hard to hire, you can use the *Hire for Grit* approach to get back to candidates immediately and ask them pertinent questions and make hiring decisions quickly. The automated engagement process creates a better candidate experience and helps with attracting the talent to your organization versus others that may take much longer to respond to candidates.

Is hiring for grit about automating the recruiter?

No! *Hire for Grit* is about empowering the recruiter. It is all about helping the recruiter and talent acquisition team work better, be more productive, and focus on finding the talent that can help any organization excel. The strategies that we have discussed helps recruiters be better at what they do. For example:

1. *Hire for Grit* helps recruiters widen the recruiting funnel without taking on more of a workload.
2. *Hire for Grit* helps engage the talent in a way that helps scale how a recruiter "sells" the company to candidates.
3. *Hire for Grit* allows a recruiter to dig out of the avalanche of resumes in seconds! Imagine being able to zero-in on the candidates that are most suited for the role based on their effort, interest, and capabilities.
4. *Hire for Grit* also helps recruiters to collaborate better with hiring managers and others that are part of the hiring process.

At first, most changes or different ways of working in a role may lead to the feeling that you are losing control. Yet one must remember that the only thing that is constant in life is change. The sooner recruiters embrace the *Hire for Grit* approach the faster they are able to focus on creating an amazing experience for candidates and attracting them to join their team.

ACKNOWLEDGMENTS

———

I'd like to acknowledge those who made this book possible. I was just the author, but behind the scenes many supported, guided, and encouraged me to keep moving forward with grit and gratitude:

My parents, wife, son, daughter, brother, sister, mother-in-law, sister-in-law and brother-in-law; thank you for always unconditionally supporting me.

Eric Koester who unconditionally supports first time authors.

Bianca daSilva without whom I would be lost in this arduous book writing process.

The entire New Degree Press team for giving me a chance to write.

Pete Lyons, Jay Laabs, David Adkins, Alicia Kenney, Ranga Venkatesan, Ben Gawiser, Jason Arbegast, Paul Greenland, Jeremy Epstein, Farhan Thawar, Glenn Jackson, Peter Mazoff,

Cara Halladay, Alex Villafranca, Mason Argiropoulos for sharing your stories about hiring for grit.

Paul Seminara who has been my friend and mentor at GRITSEED.

My current team at GRITSEED who pushes forward every day against all odds.

The entire crew from Cloud62 and my family at Huron Consulting Group.

My friend, Beejesh, for listening and always giving me candid feedback.

Visionaries who believed in hiring for grit & GRITSEED long before I wrote this book:

Mayor Restaino, Steve Davis, Tom Hayes, Mike Colyer, Nagendra Raina, Dave Austin, Bobbie Zimkowski, Dan Magnuszewski, Pat Whalen, Lou Nuchereno, David Beaton, John Doyle, Ty Hookway, Eric Pleskow, Doug Elia, Stephanie Argentine and Jenn Goodson.

I'd also like to gratefully acknowledge the following people for graciously supporting this book:

Patrick Whalen, Moshim Kukar, Mario Desiderio, Ravi Prasad, Scott Falbo, Patrick O'Brien, Satnam Basra, Nitin Arora, Maulik Kotak, Surjit Padham, Shilpa Pattani, Ben Lubetsky, Nagendra Raina, Ben Pearce, Tom Engelhardt, Mitesh Suchak, Mary Ellen Frandina, Amandeep Pal, Manny

Varma, Beejesh Kanabar, Mandeep Singh, Sachin Ruparelia, Sahil Kotecha, Melanie DellaPietra, Gaurav Kotak, William Dever, Sachin Wadhawan, Sanjay Chadha, Julia Stoklosa, Christine O'Rourke Brady, Joe Wiley, Prashant Pendyala, Akash Parashar, Rajan Kalra, Ben Gawiser, Param Singh, Alpesh Shah, C. Michael Zabel, Vikram Sodhi, Raman Sood, Mandar Deshpande, Tina Babhra, Sarju Batavia, Vic Singh, Raj Cheruvu, Jay Laabs, Arpan Lidder, Rachel Savage, John Cherry, Michael Bene, Thomas Murdock, Paul Seminara, Martin K. Casstevens, Kimberly Kohl, John A. Howard, Monica Summers, Lynnel Herrera-Ross, Mei Liu, Snehal Tanna, Julia Pastor, Tomislav Vrljicak, Erik Gregory, Sadhna Gupta, James Andre LaCour, Matt Dennis, Ryan Gudis, Tom Sabbag, Stephanie Argentine, Warren Mangahas, Vishal Sharma, Kevin Neary, Hugh Russ, Akruti Babaria, Scott McBride, John Bridges, Nasir Ali, Minesh Patel, Nancy Erwin, Syed Ali Raza, John Doyle, Nazca Fontes, Rich Burke, Raj Kalyandurg, Rajinder Bajwa, Andrew C Bearese, Doug Buerkle, Peter Lyons, Taylor Atkinson, Susan Kernan, Pranay Paw, Matt Orszewski, Eric Koester, Whitney Skeans, Jonathan C Dunsmoor, Richard Amantia II, Thomas Hayes, James Partsch Jr, Jack Greco, Alisa Sciolino, Lorenz Gan, Scott Stenclik, Dan Franasiak, Matthew Schiavi, Paul Tang, Kendall Priebe, Suresh Dasani, Zach Lees, Alexander Schuster, Jeff Parish, Jennifer Kelchlin, Dan Magnuszewski, Marty Bergerson, Vrahram Kadkhodaian, Eric Tomasini, Courtney Cannata

APPENDIX

Introduction

Gantz, John F. *The Salesforce Economy Forecast: 3.3 Million New Jobs and $859 Billion New Business Revenue to Be Created from 2016 to 2022*. Framingham: International Data Corporation, 2017. https://www.salesforce.com/content/dam/web/en_us/www/documents/white-papers/idc-study-salesforce-economy.pdf.

Gerdman, Dina. "Minorities Who 'Whiten' Job Resumes Get More Interviews." *Working Knowledge* (blog). *Harvard Business School*, May 17, 2017. https://hbswk.hbs.edu/item/minorities-who-whiten-job-resumes-get-more-interviews.

Kesler, Judd B., Corinne Low, and Colin D. Sullivan. "Incentivized Resume Rating: Eliciting Employer Preferences without Deception." *National Bureau of Economic Research*, (May 2019). http://www.nber.org/papers/w25800.

Nash, Kim S. "CIOs Get Clever about Finding Needed Skills as IT Talent Shortage Grows." *CIO Blog. Wall Street Journal*, May 19, 2015. https://www.wsj.com/articles/BL-CIOB-7110.

Owens, Sean. *The Total Economic Impact™ of Microsoft Azure IaaS: Cost Savings, New Revenue Opportunities, and Business*

Benefits Enabled by Azure IaaS. Cambridge, MA: Forrester Research, 2017. https://4aknpe3aqbbr46ba2p3cyypr-wpengine.netdna-ssl. com/wp-content/uploads/2018/06/Azure-IaaS-Total-Economic-Impact-Report-TEI-2017-by-Forrester.pdf.

UCLA Newsroom. "UCLA Study Suggests Researchers Look More Closely at Connections between Names and Race." UCLA Newsroom press release, September 8, 2017. UCLA Newsroom website. Written by Jessica Wolf. https://newsroom.ucla.edu/releases/ucla-study-suggests-researchers-look-more-closely-at-connections-between-names-and-race, accessed February 27, 2020.

Chapter 1

Desjardins, Jeff. *Which Companies Make the Most Revenue per Employee?*. Vancouver, BC: Visual Capitalist, 2017. Figure 1. https://www.visualcapitalist.com/companies-revenue-per-employee/.

Gaucher, Danielle, Justin Friesen, and Aaron C. Kay. "Evidence That Gendered Wording in Job Advertisements Exists and Sustains Gender Inequality." *Journal of Personality and Social Psychology* 101, no. 1 (January 2011): 109-28. https://gap.hks.harvard.edu/evidence-gendered-wording-job-advertisements-exists-and-sustains-gender-inequality.

Goldin, Claudia and Cecelia Rouse. "Orchestrating Impartiality: The Impact of 'Blind' Auditions on Female Musicians." *American Economic Review* 90, no. 4 (September 2000): 715-741. https://doi.org/10.1257/aer.90.4.715.

Johnson Hess, Abigail. "How to Land a Job at Mckinsey." *Make It* (blog). *CNBC*, June 6, 2018. https://www.cnbc.com/2018/06/06/

how-to-land-a-job-at-mckinsey.html.

Knight, Rebecca. "7 Practical Ways to Reduce Bias in Your Hiring Process." *Talent Acquisition* (blog). *Society for Human Resource Management*, April 19, 2018. https://www.shrm.org/resourcesandtools/hr-topics/talent-acquisition/pages/7-practical-ways-to-reduce-bias-in-your-hiring-process.aspx.

Krumrie, Matt. "Why Candidates Never Hear Back from Hiring Managers." *Zip Recruiter Blog*, July 6, 2015. https://www.ziprecruiter.com/blog/why-candidates-never-hear-back-from-hiring-managers/.

Mariotti, Andrew, Sam Robinson, and Evren Esen. *2017 Talent Acquisition Benchmarking Report*. Alexandria, VA: Society for Human Resource, 2017. https://www.shrm.org/hr-today/trends-and-forecasting/research-and-surveys/Documents/2017-Talent-Acquisition-Benchmarking.pdf.

Mohr, Tara Sophia. "Why Women Don't Apply for Jobs Unless They're 100% Qualified." *Harvard Business Review*, August 25, 2014. https://hbr.org/2014/08/why-women-dont-apply-for-jobs-unless-theyre-100-qualified.

Northwestern University. "The Cost of a Bad Hire." *Northwestern*, February 2019. https://www.northwestern.edu/hr/about/news/february-2019/the-cost-of-a-bad-hire.html.

Peterson, Thad. "Top CEO Priorities in 2019." *Consultant Resources* (blog). *The Predictive Index*, accessed February 28, 2021. https://www.predictiveindex.com/blog/top-ceo-priorities-in-2019/.

Smith, Clive. "I Was a Recruiter for Goldman Sachs. Here's Who They Want to Hire." *eFinancialCareers* (blog), May 5, 2016. https://www.efinancialcareers.com/news/finance/getting-a-job-at-goldman-sachs.

Umoh, Ruth. "Top Google Recruiter: Google Uses This 'Shocking' Strategy to Hire the Best Employees." *Make It* (blog). *CNBC*, January 10, 2018. https://www.cnbc.com/2018/01/10/google-uses-this-shocking-strategy-to-hire-the-best-employees.html.

U.S. Bureau of Labour Statistics. *Job Openings Levels and Rates by Industry and Region, Seasonally Adjusted*. February 9, 2021, Economic News Release distributed by U.S. Bureau of Labour Statistics. Accessed January 16, 2021. https://www.bls.gov/news.release/jolts.to1.htm.

Wharton University. "Uncovering Bias: A New Way to Study Hiring Can Help." *Knowledge@Wharton* (blog). *Wharton School of the University of Pennsylvania*, July 18, 2019. https://knowledge.wharton.upenn.edu/article/uncovering-hiring-bias/.

Chapter 2

Clear, James. "Grit: A Complete Guide on Being Mentally Tough." *James Clear* (blog). Accessed on February 28, 2021. https://jamesclear.com/grit.

Duckworth, Angela. "Grit Passion and Perseverance for Long-Term Goals." Character Lab. Accessed on February 28, 2021. https://characterlab.org/playbooks/grit/.

Duckworth, Angela. "Grit: The Power of Passion and Perseverance." Filmed April 2013 in New York, NY. TED video, 2:55. https://www.ted.com/talks/angela lee duckworth grit the power of passion and perseverance/up-next?language=en.

Duckworth, Angela. *Grit: The Power of Passion and Perseverance*. New York: Charles Scribner's Sons, 2016.

Fortune. "100 Best Companies to Work for." Accessed on February 28, 2021. https://fortune.com/best-companies/2020/search/.

Chapter 3

Benioff, Marc. "Create Strategic Company Alignment with a V2MOM." *The 360 Blog. Salesforce.com*, May 1, 2020. https://www.salesforce.com/blog/how-to-create-alignment-within-your-company/.

Dillon Thomson. "Elon Musk Makes Surprising Tesla Recruiting Pitch: 'I Don't Care If You Even Graduated High School'." *In The Know* (blog). *Yahoo Life*, May 1, 2020. https://www.yahoo.com/lifestyle/2020-02-04-elon-musk-tesla-hiring-high-schoool-artifical-intelligence-party-twitter-23918679.html.

Henry, Zoë. "How Richard Branson Hires Remarkable People: 3 Rules." *Icons & Innovators* (blog). *Inc Magazine*, March 27, 2015. https://www.inc.com/zoe-henry/3-tips-from-richard-branson-for-hiring-remarkable-people.html.

Williams, Ray. "The Biggest Predictor of Career Success? Not Skills or Education—but Emotional Intelligence." *Financial Post*, January 1, 2014. https://financialpost.com/executive/careers/the-biggest-predictor-of-career-success-not-skills-or-education-but-emotional-intelligence.

Chapter 4

Biro, Meghan M. "Top 5 Reasons You Never Hear Back after Applying for a Job." *Career Advice* (blog). *Glassdoor*, February 3, 2020. https://www.glassdoor.com/blog/top-5-reasons-hear-applying-job/.

Chamorro-Premuzic, Tomas. "True Long-Term Career Success Depends on This Most Underrated Aspect of Talent." *Fast Company Magazine*, October 7, 2019. https://www.fastcompany.com/90413553/true-long-term-career-success-depends-on-this-most-under-rated-aspect-of-talent.

Conlan, Catherine. "Survey Finds Millions of Americans Are Underemployed." *Advice* (blog). *Monster.com*, accessed March 1, 2021. https://www.monster.com/career-advice/article/millions-americans-underemployed-0820.

Federal Reserve Bank of New York. *The Labor Market for Recent College Graduates*. New York: Federal Reserve Bank of New York, 2021. https://www.newyorkfed.org/research/college-labor-market/index.html.

Gould, Elise, Zane Mokhiber, and Julia Wolfe. *Class of 2019 College Edition*. Washington, DC: Economic Policy Institute, 2019. https://www.epi.org/publication/class-of-2019-college-edition/.

Morgan, Steve. "Humans on the Internet Will Triple from 2015 to 2022 and Hit 6 Billion." *Cybercrime Magazine*, July 18, 2019. https://cybersecurityventures.com/how-many-internet-users-will-the-world-have-in-2022-and-in-2030/.

Renub Research. *Online Education Market & Global Forecast, by End User, Learning Mode (Self-Paced, Instructor LED), Technology, Country, Company*. United States: Renub Research, 2019. https://www.researchandmarkets.com/reports/4876815/online-education-market-and-global-forecast-by.

Wei, Lu, and Douglas Hindman. "Does the Digital Divide Matter More? Comparing the Effects of New Media and Old Media Use on the Education-Based Knowledge Gap." *Mass Communication & Society* 14, no. 2 (February 2011): 216-235. https://doi.org/10.1080/15205431003642707.

Chapter 5

Pemberton, Chris. *Tap into the Marketing Power of SMS*. Stamford, CT: Gartner, 2016. https://www.gartner.com/en/marketing/insights/articles/tap-into-the-marketing-power-of-sms.

Chapter 6

Campbell, Mikey. "Half of New Apple's US Hires in 2018 Lacked 4-Year College Degrees, Cook Says." *Apple Insider* (blog), 2020. https://appleinsider.com/articles/19/03/06/half-of-new-apples-us-hires-in-2018-lacked-4-year-college-degrees-cook-says

Gaucher, Danielle, Justin Friesen, and Aaron C. Kay. "Evidence That Gendered Wording in Job Advertisements Exists and Sustains Gender Inequality." *Journal of Personality and Social Psychology* 101, no. 1 (January 2011): 109-28. https://doi.apa.org/doi/10.1037/a0022530.

Hastings, Reed. "Freedom and Responsibility Culture." Poster presented online at Slideshare.com, 2009. https://www.slideshare.net/reed2001/culture-2009.

Human Network Contributor. "The Latest Stats on Women in Tech." *ICT Solutions & Education*, October 1, 2020. https://www.isemag.com/2020/10/telecom-the-latest-stats-on-women-in-tech/.

Matfield, Kat. "Gender Decoder for Job Ads." Gender Decoder, November 5, 2018. http://gender-decoder.katmatfield.com/about.

Mohr, Tara Sophia. "Why Women Don't Apply for Jobs Unless They're 100% Qualified." *Harvard Business Review*, August 25, 2014. https://hbr.org/2014/08/why-women-dont-apply-for-jobs-unless-theyre-100-qualified.

Netflix. "Netflix Jobs." Accessed February 28, 2021. https://jobs.netflix.com.

Peretz, Marissa. "The Job Description Is Obsolete." *Forbes*, June 13, 2018. https://www.forbes.com/sites/marissaperetz/2018/06/13/the-job-description-is-obsolete/?sh=1bc0f08575b8.

Shepardson, David. "CEOs Tell Trump They Are Hiring More Americans without College Degrees." Aerospace & Defense, *Reuters*, March 6, 2019. https://www.reuters.com/article/

us-usa-trump-workforce/ceos-tell-trump-they-are-hiring-more-americans-without-college-degrees-idUSKCN1QN2XO.

Chapter 7

Indeed. "Sales Development Representative." Search Results. Accessed January 22, 2021. https://www.indeed.com/viewjob?jk=e9c8e841ed98f40d&from=tp-serp&tk=1evqjinfunpe6804.

Indeed. "Software Engineer, Entry-Level." Search Results. Accessed January 22, 2021. https://www.indeed.com/viewjob?jk=06c061028ccfea3b&from=tp-serp&tk=1evqjpo9locjg801.

Laakmann, Gayle. "Is There a Link between Job Interview Performance and Job Performance?." *Forbes*, June 28, 2013. https://www.forbes.com/sites/quora/2013/06/28/is-there-a-link-between-job-interview-performance-and-job-performance/?sh=72b407fb458b.

Subramania, Jaishree. "Addressing the Coming IoT Talent Shortage." *Microsoft Industry Blogs*. Microsoft, September 16, 2019. https://cloudblogs.microsoft.com/industry-blog/manufacturing/2019/09/16/addressing-the-coming-iot-talent-shortage/.

Thawar, Farhan. "Technical Interviews Are Garbage. Here's What We Do Instead." *Medium* (blog). October 20, 2017. https://medium.com/helpful-com/https-medium-com-fnthawar-helpful-technical-interviews-are-garbage-dc5d9aee5acd.

Chapter 8

Ramirez, Fernando. "5 Compelling Statistics about Recruiting Behavior." *Recruiting* (blog). *Recruiter.com*, September 16,

2014. https://www.recruiter.com/i/5-compelling-statistics-about-recruiting-behavior/.

Chapter 9

Chamberlain, Dr. Andrew. "How Long Does It Take to Hire? Interview Duration in 25 Countries." *Economic Research* (blog). *Glassdoor*, August 9, 2017. https://www.glassdoor.com/research/time-to-hire-in-25-countries/.

Miaskoff, Carol R. "EEOC Informal Discussion Letter." U.S. Equal Employment Opportunity Commission. Last modified November 4, 2010. https://www.eeoc.gov/foia/eeoc-informal-discussion-letter-213.

Society of Human Resource Managment. "Average Cost-per-Hire for Companies Is $4,129, Shrm Survey Finds." SHRM press release, August 3, 2016. https://www.shrm.org/about-shrm/press-room/press-releases/pages/human-capital-benchmarking-report.aspx.

Chapter 10

Goldin, Claudia and Cecelia Rouse. "Orchestrating Impartiality: The Impact of 'Blind' Auditions on Female Musicians." *American Economic Review* 90, no. 4 (September 2000): 715-741. https://doi.org/10.1257/aer.90.4.715.